PRAISE FOR THE FIRST EDITION OF STRAIGHT TALK ABOUT PUBLIC RELATIONS

Whether you're trying to write a compelling press release, pitching yourself or your product for media coverage, or creating a social media campaign that works, Robert Wynne's *Straight Talk about Public Relations* tells you everything you need to know.

> — **Dave Boone,** two-time Emmy and Writers Guild of America Award-winning writer, from the Foreword

There are too many books promising pie-in-the-sky magical social media solutions for individuals and businesses trying to conduct public relations. There are no magical apps. There is no instant gratification. Public relations is hard work. Even in the digital age, you need a great story, great connections, and a professional strategy to stand out from everyone else and break through the clutter. Robert Wynne's new book explains how public relations is different from advertising, then guides the reader through traditional methods, social media communications, and content marketing to reach journalists and other important audiences. If you're willing to work hard and want to promote yourself or your brand, read this book.

> — **Michael Levine,** public relations expert, speaker, and author of nineteen books including the bestselling *Guerrilla P.R.*

D0140131

Straight Talk is one of the few PR books I feel comfortable recommending. It's packed with actionable advice, great tips from a wealth of experts, and enough case studies to help professionals in a field that can use a dose of reality and a swift kick in the ass.

— **B.J. Mendelson,** author of *Social Media is Bullshit*

If Robert Wynne can persuade the media to take an interest in books written by an economist (as he did many times for me), just imagine how successful his approach would be for those of you with something genuinely interesting to say.

— **Robert H. Frank, PhD,** H. J. Louis Professor of Management and Professor of Economics at the Johnson Graduate School of Management, Cornell University, *New York Times* columnist, and bestselling author of *Success and Luck*.

An essential book for anyone who wants to understand and learn how to practice public relations.

— **Burt Lauten,** Director of Communications, Pittsburgh Steelers

This book delivers what its title promises, giving you the real scoop on what works and what doesn't in public relations. And – bonus! – it explains why PR is much more effective than advertising, at much less cost. Want to learn how PR really works? Start here.

— **Steve Tally,** Senior Strategist for STEM, Office of Public Affairs, Purdue University

Straight Talk About

PUBLIC
RELATIONS

REVISED & UPDATED

Straight Talk About

PUBLIC RELATIONS

REVISED & UPDATED

New Strategies
on Social Media and
Content Marketing

Robert Wynne

MAVEN HOUSE

Published by Maven House Press, 4 Snead Ct., Palmyra, VA 22963; 610.883.7988; www.mavenhousepress.com.

Special discounts on bulk quantities of Maven House Press books are available to corporations, professional associations, and other organizations. For details contact the publisher.

While this publication is designed to provide accurate and authoritative information in regard to the subject matter covered, it is sold with the understanding that the publisher is not engaged in rendering legal, accounting, or other professional service. If legal advice or other expert assistance is required, the services of a competent professional person should be sought.
— From the Declaration of Principles jointly adopted by a Committee of the American Bar Association and a Committee of Publishers and Associations

Library of Congress Control Number: 2018959032

Paperback ISBN: 978-1-938548-85-7
E-book ISBN: 978-1-938548-03-3

Printed in the United States of America.

To Dawn and Giovanna

Thanks for motivating me to dream big

CONTENTS

ACKNOWLEDGEMENTS

T HIS BOOK would not have been possible without the steady stream of excellent employees, interns, and independent contractors from Loyola Marymount University, UCLA, and USC who brought new ideas and energy into our public relations practice. I would also like to thank the talented communications professionals at universities, colleges, and medical schools who attend our annual media networking events. Finally, the contributions of the many reporters quoted in this book who care about journalism, democracy, and the fair exchange of ideas are extremely appreciated.

FOREWORD

For more than 20 years, I've been fortunate to count on Robert Wynne to give it to me straight. I have also counted on him for his twisted sense of humor, but let's not get ahead of ourselves.

Robert's expertise is the art of persuasion. He's a master. He even got me to write this forward. For free.

For many years, Robert has not only persuaded journalists to write glowingly about his clients, and in turn giving his clients the kind of valuable publicity that "money can't buy," he's also persuaded his clients to change their thinking, messaging, strategies, and philosophies about public relations. It's a no-nonsense approach that has worked since the days of Julius Caesar – and he became so famous that they named a casino, a salad, and a haircut after him.

PR is an art form, just like any of the art forms practiced by artists who seek a place in the public eye and the financial rewards that follow. Actors, one would hope, spend years honing their acting skills. Painters, before they touch brush to canvas, learn the craft of color-mixing, the nuances of light and shadow, style, and art history. Singers, again, one would hope, learn to sing. The art of successful PR takes the same study and discipline to master. No artist who is thrust into the public eye stays there for very long without talent combined with the proper PR machine to show it off.

Many years ago, I was getting into comedy writing while hanging out in the clubs that sprung up everywhere in the late 80s and early 90s. Comics and audiences alike were awestruck by the "overnight sensations." Those were the days when the television networks seemed to be handing out sitcoms like breath mints. Every comic I had shared late-night Buffalo wings with had a time slot on the schedule. A career in stand-up appeared to be the fast road to fame and fortune. The pages of the glossy entertainment magazines were filled with stories about current stars who abruptly walked away from their day jobs based solely on one impromptu killer set on the Sunset Strip. In nearly every office in America, the "funny guy" from accounting was probably betting that the two-minute routine he cooked up for coworkers around the break room microwave was going to be his ticket to primetime TV riches.

How often did it happen? Never. The truth is that those stories were manufactured by clever PR experts.

I recall sitting backstage with Jay Leno while we watched one such "overnight success" who had recently broken into a lucrative TV career. The story went that one night, this comic got up onstage totally unprepared and was so naturally funny that Hollywood beat down his door with contracts, Ferraris, and all the perks of being a "star." Jay looked at me and said, "Are they kidding? I've seen that guy bouncing around the clubs for more than ten years. Nothing happens overnight. You've got to work at it."

Similarly, the very talented screenwriter Shane Black famously sold his spec screenplay for *Lethal Weapon* for $250,000. His story was an interesting one. While he wasn't a complete novice, it was indeed his first big break, and he therefore seemed to come from nowhere. The ensuing mainstream publicity following his sale made nearly everyone who had ever wanted to write a movie script, and many who hadn't ever written as much as a letter, want to spend a morning drafting a script and the afternoon shopping for a mansion in Beverly Hills. And not just any mansion, one with wall-to-wall supermodels and hot and cold running cash.

Thanks to social media, more accurately *media coverage* of social media, there's a very similar culture today. The current mantra is: "Sing a song, tell a joke, improvise a scene, tweet it out, and go viral."

It's a fallacy.

For every viral sensation there are hundreds of thousands living in obscurity. While it's true that social media is currently the fastest way of getting the word out, Marshall McLuhan's famous phrase "the medium is the message" is as relevant as ever.

In straight talk terms, Robert debunks this myth that all you need to get your message out is a wacky post or silly tweet. He takes down the cyber hipsters who promote this wholly unsuccessful route to reaching an audience and keeping their attention. Social media isn't a ticket. It's a tool, just like a laptop. Neither are of much use if one doesn't have a good story to tell and the skills to tell it well. Robert does. More importantly, he's willing to share his secrets of earning and shaping public perception.

Whether you're trying to write a compelling press release, pitching yourself or your product for media coverage, or creating a social media campaign that works, Robert Wynne's *Straight Talk about Public Relations* tells you everything you need to know. And I'm happy to say that his twisted sense of humor is intact and splattered all over the pages that follow.

Dave Boone

INTRODUCTION

W<small>HAT IS PUBLIC RELATIONS?</small>
It's a concept that vexes most people in America. The vast majority confuse it with advertising.

There's something sexy about advertising. It's cool. A group of men and women sit around a mahogany boardroom table in Manhattan with the Empire State Building casting shadows on their chiseled faces. Sipping martinis and smoking cigarettes, they watch big screens with colorful images of perfect people enjoying perfect products.

They briefly debate catchy taglines, then someone, usually wearing a trendy outfit with a rakish tie or purple scarf, delivers a witty idea, and everyone smiles. After a few knowing nods where everyone congratulates themselves for being so insightful, the group breaks into applause. These are the pictures, stories, and films that will please consumers and fatten the wallets of clients. These are the concepts that everyone will love.

Cool.

Just one problem with this scene straight out of the TV show *Mad Men* or the hundreds of precursors and movie scenes just like it. As consumers, we're conditioned to ignore advertising. Advertising, on its own, rarely works.

Remember those "Got Milk" ads on TV and in print that ran for years? Most people do. They had a 90 percent familiarity rate with adults. Celebrities with the milk moustache appeared in every magazine and TV show. But the campaign, like most advertisements, failed. From 1995, when it debuted, to 2011, yearly milk consumption for adults declined from 23.9 gallons to 20. Oops!

Before anyone cries over all those gallons of spilled milk, the advertising industry doesn't need to worry about failing. According to *Fortune* magazine, U.S. firms spend $150 billion a year on advertising vs. only $5 billion for public relations.

Why is that?

Part of it is habit. When General Motors went broke in 2009 they were one of the biggest advertisers on TV. When GM emerged from bankruptcy and reorganized a few months later, guess how they promoted their cars? Advertising. Auto manufacturing is an old business, with old habits. The other reason to continue advertising is control. With advertising, clients directly control the message.

Public relations is less direct and more subtle. There are filters. To get your messages into print media or on other media such as influential websites, TV, or radio, someone must be convinced, or persuaded, rather than purchased.

Contrast images in the media of public relations professionals and ad people. These portrayals are rarely accurate and hardly representative. Most PR characters are women like Samantha of *Sex and the City,* event planners more concerned with celebrities, the right shade of lipstick, martini recipes, and brand of high heels than in promoting their clients. Or Olivia Pope in *Scandal,* who magically snaps her fingers, walks through layers of security into closed TV studios and Congress, and instantly conjures talking points and strategy while pitting media outlets against each other to further her agenda. The stories she plants run within minutes, sometimes seconds.

Shauna Roberts, the trash-talking celebrity publicist for Vince in *Entourage,* represents another media cliché, the aggressive bulldog and mothering character who saves her client from himself while battling the forces of the paparazzi.

Events, crisis management, and celebrity spin are part of the PR business. But it's probably a fraction of what most professionals do every day. Public relations is the persuasion business. It's not easy. It's not instant. It's seldom glamorous. Most people work for themselves or for corporations or small businesses, providing services or selling insurance, coffee, software, auto parts, or millions of other everyday products. The PR folks at these companies don't plan trendy parties, hang out with rock stars, or waltz into the Senate.

For most of the world, public relations is convincing customers to visit a website or store, to buy a product, to support a local candidate, to agree with a position on the new factory or park. In simple terms, public relations is persuasion created to mobilize an audience to take a certain action.

This book separates fact from fiction, reality from fantasy. People who think they can learn "Five Magical Secrets for Tweeting to Make You a Millionaire in Five Minutes or Less" will be disappointed (although there are plenty of books and websites that promise these services).

There are five chapters in this book: (1) Public Relations, with lessons on how to perform the specific functions to help promote products and causes, anecdotes on successful PR campaigns, and knowledge about how the news is created and influenced; (2) Social Media, featuring practices, definitions, and strategies to understand the limitations and benefits of various platforms; (3) Content Marketing, so professionals can study the best practices of self-published posts, articles, videos, and other forms of communications and the best way to promote them; (4) Measurement, with standards and techniques to gauge the impact of PR efforts; and (5) Top Five PR Campaigns, featuring examples of amazing, successful PR campaigns.

Public relations isn't easy. It can't be learned at a party, on social media while sipping lattes at a trendy coffee bistro, or even in a classroom. Influencing audiences and leaders is hard work.

Let's begin.

CHAPTER 1

Public Relations

*If you would persuade, you must appeal to
interest rather than intellect.*
— Benjamin Franklin

JULIUS CAESAR WAS HAVING A GREAT YEAR.
The Roman general, politician, and statesman was kicking ass in 58 BC with his military campaign in Gaul. In a great battle, he repelled the Helvetii and pushed them back to Switzerland. After defeating the Helvetians, Caesar marched against the leader Ariovistus and repelled those forces across the Rhine. In just eight years he conquered the entire province of Gaul, an area comprising modern-day France, Belgium, and Germany.

But the general had a big problem. Back in Rome, the aristocratic elite believed Caesar (100 BC–45 BC) was too ambitious and interested in self-glory. Word came that not only his position but his life might be in danger. Without the support of the masses – the Roman plebians – he would be returned to Rome covered in chains, not glory.

So what did Caesar do? He wrote a book. Eight of them, in fact.

His tremendous success on the battlefield was publicized and communicated to the elites in government and the masses via several books of commentary, *Commentarii*, which were public reports concerning his military victories in Gaul, modern-day France.

"One of the main themes of Caesar's famous war commentaries was to show how each campaign was in the best interests of the republic," notes the History Channel. "The commentaries were most likely published a book at a time, each one written and released in the winter months after each campaign, all depicting the author as a distinguished and loyal servant of the republic."

Julius Caesar was one of the first practitioners of public relations. He successfully leveraged the power of public opinion and patriotism to advance the interests of Rome while furthering his military, political, and personal goals. His efforts exemplified several essential truths. Public relations is powerful. Public relations is like plutonium – it can be used for good or evil. It's basically amoral, not concerned with questions of right or wrong. What one person or group considers righteous can be interpreted as unethical by someone else.

Communications throughout history have disguised, as benefits to the public, actions that were designed to enrich and empower the elite while harming the masses. But there are just as many public relations efforts that honestly promote the general goodwill. Wars, highway construction, fluoride in the water, smoking advocacy, voting rights, charitable campaigns, elections – all of them are

What Public Relations Has Been Called

- Promotion
- Advocacy
- Persuasion
- Coercion
- Brainwashing

- Spin
- Arm-twisting
- Lobbying
- Propaganda
- Duplicity

- Manipulation
- Influence peddling
- Consensus building
- Cajolery
- Humbuggery

Figure 1.1. Various terms that have been used to describe public relations. In fact, public relations consists of a bit of each of them.

accompanied by PR campaigns, usually on both sides of the issue. It's the nature of the art of PR.

Public relations has been called many things – see Figure 1.1 for a few of them. It uses all of the elements listed, and more. In its most basic form, its purest crystal, PR is the *persuasion business.* It involves advocacy by trying to convince an audience, inside your group or from the outside world, to agree with or not oppose your position. It could involve the promotion of an idea, the purchase of a product, supporting a candidate, taking a specific action, choosing a policy position, or the recognition of an accomplishment to enhance the stature of a person, group, city, or country.

PR isn't easy. Do you change your opinions frequently? Do you find it easy to convince your family, friends, or co-workers to vote for a new candidate, try a different product, or modify their habits? Now try persuasion on a grand scale. That's public relations.

Books promising new paradigms, quick solutions, magical tweets, and instant gratification will disappoint the reader. Posts, tweets, snapchats, random thoughts, and cute photos rarely, if ever, move the needle. For every rock star, political movement, or product virally launched via social media, there are billions of daily electronic messages completely ignored.

PR isn't easy.

Public Relations Defined

The Public Relations Society of America (PRSA), the official group of the industry, solicited thousands of contributions for the official definition of *public relations*. The responses led to this boilerplate: "Public relations is a strategic communication process that builds mutually beneficial relationships between organizations and their publics."

In utopia, this would be true. It's a noble effort at using PR to improve the perception of PR. PRSA goes on to describe the actual functions of PR in a little more detail:

- Anticipating, analyzing, and interpreting public opinion, attitudes, and issues that might impact, for good or ill, the operations and plans of the organization.

- Counseling management at all levels in the organization with regard to policy decisions, courses of action, and communication, taking into account their public ramifications and the organization's social or citizenship responsibilities.

- Researching, conducting, and evaluating, on a continuing basis, programs of action and communication to achieve the informed public understanding necessary to the success of an organization's aims. These may include marketing; financial; fund raising; employee, community, or government relations; and other programs.

- Planning and implementing the organization's efforts to influence or change public policy. Setting objectives, planning, budgeting, recruiting and training staff, developing facilities – in short, managing the resources needed to perform all of the above.

The Princeton Review defines it much better: "A public relations specialist is an image shaper. Their job is to generate positive publicity for their client and enhance their reputation. . . . They keep the public informed about the activity of government agencies, explain policy, and manage political campaigns. Public relations people working for a company may handle consumer relations, or the relationship between parts of the company such as managers and employees, or different branch offices."

The Beginnings of Public Relations

Humans are social animals. Ever since we gathered in small families, then groups, forming towns, cities, and states, there was a need to unite the majority behind ideas or actions. Move to a new location, hunt a certain animal, fight another tribe, plant crops, build a pyramid, or sail a big ship. Of course, in ancient times nobody wrote press releases, stood on a soapbox, or, until recently, even used soap (the widespread use of soap was launched by public relations campaigns in the 1920s by Ivory Soap).

The beginnings of public relations are somewhat murky. Since people learned to speak a common language, the craftiest leaders were persuaders, seducers, influencers, and builders of consensus. Besides Julius Caesar, other leaders through the ages understood the power of the people. Napoleon Bonaparte (1769–1821), the Emperor of France, recognized the importance of persuading the masses as the key to his power. He said, "Do you know what amazes me more than anything else? The impotence of force to organize anything."

Public relations has been utilized throughout history to justify war, taxes, treaties, alliances, building bridges and monuments, and most government functions.

Early Public Relations in the United States

Thomas Jefferson

In 1807, Thomas Jefferson used the term in his Seventh Address to Congress. "Whether what shall remain of this, with the future surpluses, may be usefully applied to purposes already authorized or more usefully to others requiring new authorities, or how otherwise they shall be disposed of, are questions calling for the notice of Congress, unless, indeed, they shall be superseded by a change in our *public relations* now awaiting the determination of others." [italics mine]

The prescience of Jefferson in the practice of mass persuasion, along with most of the Founding Fathers, is superseded only by the stilting formality of the speech. No one would compare it to "Ask not what your country can do for you," "Tear down this wall," "It's the economy, stupid," or "We are the change that we seek." But in 1807 Jefferson's prose accomplished its goals.

P. T. Barnum

Some of the bad reputation of public relations emanates from one of the masters of manipulation, P.T. Barnum (1810–1891). Barnum's actions, deeds, and quotes still resonate today more than a century after his death.

A businessman, showman, and politician, he's best remembered for Barnum's American Museum in New York, which showcased such curiosities as live animals from Africa, bearded ladies, fake skeletons of mermaids, and more oddities. His name lives on today with Ringling Bros. and Barnum & Bailey's Circus, which introduced the traveling three-ring circus to America. According to *The Great and Only Barnum* by Candace Fleming, it was not only the biggest and best of the day but the first to use railroad cars to transport its acrobats, magicians, and animals, greatly expanding its range of audiences, and profits.

Barnum – The World's Greatest Showman – promoted, titillated, shocked, and outright lied to the press and the public. Notable stunts included exhibiting an African-American slave who allegedly served as the maid to George Washington. She was supposed to be 161 years old. After months of duping the public, who paid to see the woman up close, it was revealed during an autopsy (for which Barnum sold tickets) that she was only 80 years old. She had never met the founding father.

Barnum famously said "Controversy is good for business," "Every crowd has a silver lining," and "Without promotion something terrible happens . . . nothing!" He's also credited with the phrase, "There's a sucker born every minute," but that was more likely uttered by a journalist who described the audience attending one of Barnum's events. The term *humbug* or *humbuggery* is attributed to Barnum, who used the phrase to describe what he believed was a harmless stunt, not an outright lie.

Barnum was clearly one of the greatest promoters in history, but he wasn't the father of public relations. That title is usually shared by Ivy Ledbetter Lee and Edward Bernays.

The Father of Public Relations

Ivy Lee (1877–1934) and Edward Bernays (1891–1995) are to public relations what Isaac Newton and Albert Einstein are to physics. Newton famously said that he "stood on the shoulders of giants" to explain his breathtaking discoveries. Lee and Bernays invented and refined so many communications concepts that they are the giants whose shoulders we stand upon today. They elevated the reputations and multiplied the influence of clients ranging from the U.S. government and the Red Cross to Lucky Strike cigarettes, from Ivory Soap to John D. Rockefeller and Standard Oil, from the Pennsylvania Railroad to the Soviet Union (remember, public relations is amoral).

Concepts and tactics such as press releases, fact sheets, and expert testimonials seem common and ordinary today because they're so widely used. But they were revolutionary when first used by Lee and Bernays. They created a series of earthquakes in communications, repositioning relationships between large corporations, the media, and the public. They displayed rare genius in their knowledge of human psychology and desire, evolving wants into needs by manipulating large audiences and the public, not only to accept the ideas or products of their clients but to demand them.

Lee and Bernays both started out as reporters in New York, where they learned the business of journalism and developed an understanding of the needs of reporters and their publications or stations.

Ivy Lee

Ivy Lee began his career reporting for the *New York American,* the *New York Times,* and the *New York World.* Tired of the low pay and long hours, in 1903 he transitioned from journalism to "press agentry." At his own agency, in 1906, he tried to elevate the poor reputation of his industry while increasing efficiency via his "Declaration of Principles." A master of the humble-brag, the declaration proved to be both self-serving and hugely beneficial to the relationship between the media and his clients, mostly large corporations.

Ivey Lee declared, "This is not a secret press bureau. All our work is done in the open. We aim to supply news. This is not an advertising agency. If you think any of our matter ought to properly go to your business office, do not use it. Our matter is accurate. Further details on any subject treated will be supplied promptly, and any editor will be assisted most carefully in verifying directly any statement of fact. . . . In brief our plan is frankly, and openly, on behalf of business concerns and public institutions to supply the press and public of the United States prompt and accurate information concerning subjects which it is of value and interest to the public to know about."

Lee practiced what he preached concerning a deadly accident in Atlantic City, in 1906, on the Pennsylvania railroad. Instead of following the usual practices of denial, obfuscation, and outright lying about the cause of the crash, number of victims, and other facts, Lee convinced his clients to open the crash site to reporters. According to the website Behind the Spin and information from public relations classes at Buffalo State University, Lee distributed fact sheets and made executives available to speak to journalists on the record. In doing so, Lee created a field of public relations known as crisis communications.

The American Red Cross benefited from Lee's counsel as he significantly bolstered the recognition of the charity, elevating it among hundreds of competitors by using hard facts, statistical data, and human interest stories, which were innovative tactics for their time. Another client included John D. Rockefeller, the chairman of Standard Oil and "the most hated man in America." *The Unseen Power: Public Relations: A History* by Scott M. Cutlip notes that Lee made Rockefeller seem more charitable and humane. Tactics included sending him to visit the camps of strikers in his coal mines, where he was photographed talking and sharing meals with them.

This was very different from Rockefeller's previous tactics, which included using goons to beat up and occasionally shoot at the strikers.

Lee's career ended abruptly, and partially in scandal. In 1934, he was testifying at a congressional hearing that was investigating his representation of IG Farben, a controversial German chemical company that cooperated with Nazi officials. During the hearing he died, at age 57, of a brain

Figure 1.2. Ivy Lee (right) and Edward Bernays (left) have both been described as the father of public relations.

tumor. Although Lee was never shown to have contributed to the Nazi cause, his reputation took a beating.

Edward Bernays

Edward Bernays had the good fortune to live a long life, and he constantly promoted his own image in addition to those of his clients. The nephew of the world-famous psychotherapist Sigmund Freud, Bernays was born in Austria but raised in the United States. In 1990, *Life* magazine named Bernays one of the 100 "Most Influential Americans in the 20th Century."

Too short to become a soldier in World War I, Bernays volunteered to join Woodrow Wilson's Committee on Public Information (CPI), a propaganda agency engaged in promoting the war domestically and in publicizing American war aims abroad. He's credited with creating the phrase "Make the World Safe for Democracy."

"Bernays and journalistic giant Walter Lippman came to Woodrow Wilson's aid in 1917 to reverse negative public sentiment about war. These two behind-the-curtain wizards were indispensable in helping the president whip gun-shy America into an anti-German frenzy to go 'over there for WWI,'" according to James Sandrolini in *Propaganda: The Art of War*. "Bernays took propaganda seriously for his career work: he combined individual and social psychology, public opinion studies, political persuasion, and advertising to construct 'necessary illusions,' which filtered out to the masses as 'reality.'"

Bernays is the author of three classic books: *Crystallizing Public Opinion*, 1923; *Propaganda*, 1928; and *The Engineering of Consent*, 1955. By any measurement, *Propaganda* is a masterwork that influenced governments, corporations, and individuals, including Nazis such as Joseph Goebbels, the image shaper to Adolf Hitler. Bernays was Jewish, but that didn't matter to Goebbels. The observations noted in *Propaganda* include: "Whatever social importance is done today, whether in politics, finance, manufacture, agriculture, charity, education, or other fields, must be done with the help of propaganda. Propaganda is the executive arm of the invisible government."

Despite the negative connotations of the word *propaganda*, Bernays believed he was part of a small, benevolent elite that manipulated public opinion for the greater good. Bernays said, "The conscious and intelligent manipulation of the organized habits and opinions of the masses is an important element in democratic society. Those who manipulate this unseen mechanism of society constitute an invisible government which is the true ruling power of our country. We are governed, our minds molded, our tastes formed, our ideas suggested, largely by men we have never heard of. This is a logical result of the way in which our democratic society is organized. Vast numbers of human beings must cooperate in this manner if they are to live together as a smoothly functioning society."

A few of the innovations he pioneered that are widely used today were mentioned in his obituary in the *New York Times*. They include:

- Using experts and opinion leaders such as doctors, scientists, and celebrities to bolster the arguments of his clients and promote their products.

- Creating publicity stunts such as women marching in public for the "right" to smoke cigarettes, a ploy he created for the American Tobacco Company in 1929. He called cigarettes "Torches of Freedom."

- Hiring focus groups to determine attitudes and prejudices.

- Using political propaganda as a tactic to promote commercial interests.

Yes, There Is a Difference Between Public Relations and Advertising

Since before Bernays and Lee and up to the present day, most people confused public relations with advertising. They still do. As a marketing employee of an Asian-based sporting goods company told me during a pitch meeting, "We don't need public relations, we are happy with our advertising agency." Unfortunately, this view is extremely common. If most people in business can't distinguish advertising from public relations, the general public must also be confused about the difference.

There's an old saying in the PR business: "Advertising is what you pay for, publicity is what you pray for." Advertising is paid media, public relations is earned media. In advertising you purchase space in a publication or on a TV program, radio show, or website – paid media – to display your message. In public relations you try to convince reporters or editors to write positive stories about you or your client, candidate, brand, or issue. Those stories appear in the editorial sections of the magazines, newspapers, TV stations, or websites, rather than the paid media sections where advertising messages appear. Your stories have more credibility because they're independently verified by trusted third parties (reporters or editors), rather than purchased.

A huge difference between PR and advertising is the return on investment. When you figure in the cost of the space or time, plus the creative design and production costs, advertising can be expensive. Adding to that cost is the fact that most advertisements need to be repeated several times before the consumer can be influenced. A former client of mine in the manufacturing sector purchased one full-page ad, in a popular weekly newsmagazine, that cost him $125,000. He expected a wave of phone calls, viral media, and multiple conversations about the ad. Instead, he got zero. Zip. Nada. In contrast, by getting quoted in

Advertising vs. Public Relations

Advertising	Public Relations
Builds exposure	Builds trust
Paid	Earned
Complete creative control	Media controls final version
Ads are mostly visual	Uses language
More expensive	Less expensive
"Buy this product"	"This is important"
Guaranteed placement	No guarantee, must persuade media
Audience is skeptical	Media gives third-party validation

Figure 1.3. Some differences between advertising and public relations.

the *New York Times, Forbes,* and by Reuters, he received invitations to speak at national events, calls from new and existing clients, and solid credibility.

In 2012, General Motors, once one of the biggest advertisers in the world, pulled all its advertisements from Facebook, concluding that their promotions didn't work at all. A decade's worth of the Got Milk campaigns resulted in higher recognition for the product, but milk sales declined significantly. As the *New Yorker* noted in 2014, "Got Milk? didn't actually get people to buy more milk." There are dozens more examples of advertisements that amuse audiences while turning off customers.

But advertising continues to dwarf public relations in total billings. Writing in *Fortune* magazine, Greg Galant of the website MuckRack noted: "Public relations is not taken seriously as a function of business or as a profession. U.S. companies spend $150 billion annually on advertising and only $5 billion on public relations, according to eMarketer and PRSA respectively. Advertising professionals make up to 75 percent more than their PR counterparts, as calculated from PayScale data."

The reasons for advertising's dominance are obvious, if not logical. Most companies are creatures of habit, and it's easier to write and pay for an advertisement than try to convince a reporter to cover them in a positive fashion. So rather than risk rejection, many entrepreneurs, small business owners, and business professionals choose advertisements – in print or on TV programs, radio shows, or online – to promote their messages. And though most advertising is ignored, at least the message "appears somewhere" and thin-skinned executives are saved from the shame of spurned advances.

"Advertising continues to embrace an antiquated, top-down, inside-out way of communicating," says Steve Cody of *Inc.* magazine. "It reflects senior management's view on what a consumer or business-to-business buyer should think is important. PR, on the other hand, depends upon listening to the conversation and understanding the who, what, when, where, why, and how of engaging in the discussion. Public relations executives excel in storytelling and, typically, present a perceived problem (e.g., childhood obesity) and their client's unique solution (e.g., a new type of fitness equipment designed by, and for, pre-teens)."

Public Relations in Action

Michael Levine, author of *Guerilla P.R.*, says the best analogy for public relations is gift wrapping, "If I went to visit a woman today and gave her a gift in a Tiffany box, it would have higher perceived value than if I just gave it to her plain. Because she and you and I live in a culture where we gift-wrap everything – our politicians, TV stars, and even our toilet paper."

A tremendous number of articles appearing in the media today are "gift-wrapped" and originate from a public relations agency. Think about it: A new smart phone. Russia hacking the American presidential election. The latest report on glaciers melting in Antarctica. These stories don't appear out of nowhere. They were written, tested, practiced, and formulated by publicists, staffers, speechwriters, or corporate experts before being sent to reporters who processed the information, rejected some assertions, accepted others, then decided to produce a news product. And then they end up in front of millions of consumers. But first the PR professionals had to get their story in front of the reporter.

Public Relations is Difficult

Obtaining a media placement consists of the following steps:

- Researching the story idea
- Writing a compelling pitch or press release

- Contacting journalists individually or via wide distribution

- Attracting the attention of the reporter

- Convincing reporters to write, broadcast, or post a relevant story

But placing stories is now harder than ever.

Most reporters work at their desks. With newspaper and magazine readership plummeting, and cable TV news viewers decreasing because of the Internet, there are a lot fewer journalists working today than 10 years ago. Instead of beating the bushes by calling sources, visiting government agencies and factories, and investigating stories the old-fashioned way, many journalists rely upon sources to feed them information – sources at companies, government agencies, industry organizations, or citizen groups. Reporters need to churn out stories more quickly than ever, and many don't have budgets or time for treasure hunts. So the ever decreasing number of journalists are inundated with information from outside sources and have little time to review what story ideas they receive, making it extremely difficult to place a story.

The Pew Research Center noted in 2014 that there are about 5.7 people working in public relations for every journalist. That number is deceiving; it's actually higher. Most entrepreneurs and small businesses don't have a full-time person handling public relations. Many don't hire a PR firm. So hundreds of thousands (if not millions) of business owners handle the duties of PR themselves. This enormous PR competition means that the limited attention of journalists is even harder to obtain.

Nothing But the Truth?

Reporters know that all sources have agendas. The best journalists are skeptical, and they understand that publicists, corporations, and governments may not always be telling the truth, the whole truth, and nothing but the truth.

The Brexit campaign, in which the British voted to leave the European Union in June 2016, is a great example. One day after the referendum passed, millions of British were Googling *European Union,* apparently ignorant of the role of the agency, what Britain's membership entailed, and what results and damages would occur upon exit. The Vote Leave campaign's biggest selling point, that the United Kingdom sent £350 million ($500 million) every week to the EU, turned out to be a lie. Red buses with the phrase "We send the EU £350 million a week – let's fund our NHS [National Health Service] instead" paraded throughout England before the vote. After Brexit passed, Vote Leave organizers admitted to the BBC that the £350 million figure was grossly inflated and there was no guarantee that the funds going to the EU as part of the membership would automatically be deposited into the NHS.

The Keystone XL Pipeline offers another good example of competing interests and completely different claims made by opposing sides. Proponents claimed that the pipeline would add 30,000 permanent jobs and restore America's energy independence, and that its construction would pose no danger to the environment. Opponents countered that once the pipeline was built, only 34 jobs would be created, most of the benefits would go to the supplier (Canada) and the main customer (China), while its construction, which was over a critical aquifer, would endanger the drinking water of millions of Americans.

The best example of the power of PR comes from the brown-nosing coverage of every single Apple product over the past 20 years. It's well-known inside the media that Steve Jobs personally called many important journalists and alternately charmed and bullied them. The brand remains incredibly valuable today thanks to his PR efforts, which continue to add value years after his death.

PR and Social Media

There are two great fallacies about using social media as a PR strategy. (More on this in the next chapter.)

- Social media is dominant; don't worry about writing and researching, just post cute short tweets and they will magically go viral with your Facebook, Instagram, and Twitter "friends" whom you've never met.

- You don't need reporters, and you don't need to do your homework on yourself, your firm, your competition, or finding the best media outlet.

Like 99.99 percent of all new apps that promise they're one-of-a-kind and better than anything ever invented, this "new" PR strategy will fail.

Here are the cold, hard facts:

- There are 205 billion emails sent each day.

- 350 million photos are posted per day on Facebook.

- 500 million tweets arrive daily.

- There are least 5.7 publicists for every journalist.

Ragan's PR Daily estimated in 2014 that there are about 1,800 press releases issued daily, based on the number of yearly releases from PR Newswire, BusinessWire, and Marketwire. That figure is probably too low, since many smaller firms send out national and local releases on their own, and new online distribution companies have popped up since then. Even a conservative guess would predict at least 2,000 releases disseminated each day, probably many more.

Unless your story is unique and you personally know a journalist or influencer, your chance of obtaining positive coverage is very low. Even with great relationships and a decent pitch, there are no magical instant-breakfast-just-add-water solutions. Stay away from junk books that talk about "winning social media campaigns in five minutes or less." The numbers are against you. There are no easy answers. Learn to practice the art of public relations. Work hard. Be persistent.

Remember the lesson of Julius Caesar, P.T. Barnum, Ivy Lee, and Edward Bernays: *It's all about the story.* Victories in Gaul. Three-ring circus. Rockefeller eating with his workers. Torches of Freedom.

A Few Tips on What Works

Although the practices of traditional PR and social media campaigns overlap significantly (press releases are often posted on Twitter, LinkedIn, etc. in addition to being distributed via email), here are a few tips that will help you with your PR campaigns.

Feature Stories: For promoting feature stories, use traditional PR methods. Social media is practically worthless.

Email and personal relationships work far better for presenting longer, in-depth feature articles. The pitches, press releases, and story information must contain a substantial number of facts, story hooks, links to current trends, and data that affect the audience. Your ultimate goal is to be the sole source of the story that's used. For that to happen, your story must include everything the media needs to make a decision to use your story. Getting an occasional quote or pairing in stories with other firms or individuals is nice. But having your feature story used is the platinum standard.

Crisis Communications: For crisis communications, use social media. Social media is much more efficient for crisis communications because information is instantly transmitted. It's ideal for communicating about accidents, elections, and real-time events.

Pitches and Press Releases: Most winning pitches and press releases are marked by at least three of the following eight characteristics of a great story:

- It offers something new
- It has human interest
- It challenges conventional wisdom
- It's visual
- It's unusual
- It's impactful
- It relates to a trend
- It's memorable

Make sure you have a great story to tell. And before reaching out to journalists, you should learn to think like a reporter. Help them reach their audience. To do that you should make sure the journalists know:

- What's the story?
- Why is it important?
- Why now?

How well that message is delivered is the key factor for your success. You must understand the story and know how to deliver that message in as few words as possible. If you can write press releases, pitch letters, and editorials well, and possess the barest of people skills, you'll never go hungry.

Bottom line: for long feature stories and most press releases and pitches, the old rules of PR still rule. So everyone in public relations should understand and master the traditional PR strategies: using press releases, pitch letters, and editorials.

Press Releases

Press releases are official documents that announce something, usually to the media, and they're meant to be posted or read somewhere in the public record. Some reasons for issuing press releases include introducing a new product or service, announcing a new location or management team, promoting an event, releasing a study or white paper, introducing changes to your business, promoting a court victory, bragging about winning an award, etc. An old saying claims that press releases save time for you and the reporter.

Unfortunately, most press releases are drier than bone. Sometimes it's because of necessity, such as when public companies have to report earnings or management changes. Sometimes it's because people don't write well. Or many times it's because a committee makes "improvements" with each draft of the release, and juice is sucked out of the orange until only the rind is left.

The Basics

Let's assume we all know the basic elements of a press release – headline, sub-headline, "For Immediate Release," date, location, inverted pyramid (most-important information first) – and the essentials of storytelling. The most important element – by far – is the headline. It frames your story and often it's the subject line of your email. If it's not interesting you don't need to worry about what follows – it will be deleted and ignored.

Imagine representing an author. She's speaking at a public school. Riveting? Not yet.

- Draft 1 – Local author speaks in front of elementary school.

- Draft 2 – Local environmental author speaks at elementary school.

- Draft 3 – Local environmental author speaks at elementary school on Earth Day . . . and teaches kids how to reduce plastic use by 30 percent.

Now the headline captures your attention.

Avoid echo headlines, where the headline says the exact same thing as the first sentence in your release. When I moved to Los Angeles in the 1990s I wrote for *Newsweek* magazine for a year. The first week on the job the bureau chief, Stryker McGuire, said he looked for three things in writing: detail, detail, detail. Pick out the specifics in your story and make them newsworthy. Dig deep. Do your homework.

Figure 1.4 shows a well-written press release by Bob Gold & Associates, a public relations firm based in Redondo Beach, California.

Let's quickly analyze the "Bricks and Bloom" release based on our checklist for the characteristics of a great story:

- It offers something new. Yes, a new sculpture.
- It has human interest. Absolutely. Kids and families can attend.
- It challenges conventional wisdom. Partially.
- It's visual. Definitely.
- It's unusual. Definitely.
- It's impactful. On a local level, yes.
- It relates to a trend. Not applicable for this one. Not every release hits every mark.
- It's memorable. Absolutely.

Press releases are distributed widely to the media via email blasts, individual emails, or press release services such as PR Newswire or PR Web. For large events and product announcements, most medium- or larger-sized firms distribute via those services for convenience and the depth and number of outlets reached. Costs range from about $100 and up for local distribution to $2,000 for national delivery including photos and/or video.

Example of A Well-Written Press Release

For Immediate Release

BRICKS AND BLOOMS MERGE FOR INTERACTIVE 'NATURE CONNECTS' FOR EXHIBIT AT SOUTH COAST BOTANIC GARDEN

Southern California's Only Stop on National Tour Connects Families to Nature with Sculptures

PALOS VERDES PENINSULA, CA (November 17, 2015) – Visitors got a chance to imagine a walk through a beautiful garden populated with bison and exotic birds today: not real ones, but magnificent sculptures constructed entirely of LEGO® bricks.

It was just a taste of the toy-filled exploration coming this spring at the South Coast Botanic Garden, which will host *Nature Connects*. This interactive art installation entirely constructed from about a quarter million toy bricks will bring 15 nature-themed sculptures to the Garden, along with multiple hands-on activities.

As the launch date for the exhibit approaches, the Garden will be hosting a family LEGO Movie Night on December 4th which includes entrance to the Garden, free popcorn and cookie decoration. Dinner will be available.

On December 26, the Garden will hold a LEGO-brick building competition for visiting children. Volunteers from regional architectural and design schools are scheduled to be at the garden to teach children how to re-envision what they build with the rectangular blocks and see how the toys can be used to form more organic shapes like arches and curves.

Figure 1.4. Sample press release written by Bob Gold & Associates.

The South Coast Botanic Garden in Palos Verdes Peninsula is the only Southern California stop for this national touring exhibit, which will be unveiled to the public on February 19. It will be on display through May 8, 2016.

"This is the first botanic garden in Southern California to offer this one-of-a-kind and engaging artistic vision, representing a whole new way to experience nature through art. In bringing *Nature Connects* to South Coast Botanic Garden, we hope to share the importance of making connections with the natural world. More importantly, with the garden's commitment to providing a unique horticultural and wildlife habitat experience, we want to demonstrate successful land reclamation and sustainability through the familiarity of LEGO toy bricks," said South Coast Botanic Garden Foundation CEO Adrienne Nakashima.

The sculptures, created by New York-based artist Sean Kenney, took seven months to build. The pieces are all incredibly detailed and assembled exclusively using the popular connecting toys. They range from a 575-piece statue of a goldfinch to a hummingbird, the symbol of the South Coast Botanic Garden, which requires 31,555 pieces and stands more than six feet tall.

Membership allows entry into the garden 364 days a year along with other exclusive perks including free parking, special members-only events and discounts. Membership covers access to this exhibition as well as admission to the Garden all year long and other benefits.

Figure 1.4 (continued). Sample press release.

What Journalists Think About Press Releases

The all-star panel of reporters listed below receives up to 1,000 emails per day, many of them press releases. You should really pay attention to what they think about press releases. After all, they're your first audience. Our panel of journalists includes:

- Jane Bornemeier, Editor, Special Sections, *New York Times*
- Jennifer Bogo, Deputy Editor, *Audubon*
- Rick Newman, Columnist, *Yahoo! Finance*
- John Biggs, Former East Coast Editor, *TechCrunch*
- Charles Fleming, Writer, *Los Angeles Times*
- Lindsey Hoshaw, Science Producer, KQED (Northern California)
- Derek Thompson, Senior Editor, *The Atlantic*
- Jason Gilbert, Former Senior Editor, *Fusion*
- Samantha Murphy Kelly, Technology Reporter, *CNN*

What could PR people do to make press releases better?

Bornemeier: The press releases that work best for me are brief, get reasonably quickly to what's new, significant and newsworthy about the event, and somehow communicate to me why a reader will find the event or announcement interesting. Does it speak to some larger issue? Why will people care about this? I appreciate press releases that have a little bit of a personal touch and demonstrate that the people writing them know why they are reaching out to me – because they know what kinds of subjects I handle – as opposed to just sending them randomly.

Bogo: First, a couple of don'ts: Please don't attach the information as a Word doc or a pdf (yes, people still do this), or merely hyperlink to a press release posted online. Don't clear your throat in the subject line – get straight to the point – and don't shout at me with all caps. I do like it when people address me personally and both include succinct information (what is it? why is it timely and important?) and point to multimedia resources.

Newman: Get to the point right away and let me know what it is in the subject line. Look up my last 20 stories (they're all in one place, on my Yahoo Finance author page) to get a feel for what I cover, and send relevant info. Send them only once. If it's a bald appeal for publicity without much substance, don't bother because you do more harm to your reputation than it's probably worth (unless of course the client is paying enough to justifying trashing your reputation).

Biggs: Nothing.

Fleming: The basics matter. Pitch me something that shows you know my publication and my area of coverage, and that you read it often enough to know that we *already did this story* a week ago. And you can go ahead and surprise me by spelling my name correctly.

Thompson: I delete most releases after about .5 seconds spent on the subject line. Make the subject line personal, the way you would if you were asking a friend a favor. Not ALL CAPS or Super Formal but casual and knowing. "Yo" has worked before to get me to open the email. "Hey Derek, wonderful piece" has worked (flattery often does for journalists!). Other than that, you have to know me and what I write about, not just pitch a story because it's about business.

Gilbert: Fix all of the things above! And press releases, unlike pitch emails, should be thorough. We're looking for all of the information about this new product or study or whatever that we can find so that we can determine if it's worth digging deeper into. Links to websites with even more information are great, too. And you *have* to have contact information at the end. And not just that, but you better be *replying* to those contacts quickly, too. Don't add an email address you never check, or a phone number for a line you never answer!

Murphy Kelly: Press releases are an efficient way to get news out to reporters, but often the language used is very dense and tedious to get through. I sometimes read an entire press release and can't pull out the key takeaway. Subjects can be complicated to begin with, especially when it comes to science and technology, so language that really cuts to the chase and explains the news is most helpful. I always like to say, explain it to me in a sentence or two like you were telling your grandmother, before getting into the specifics. It's always good to know why the news is important too — if it's not my main area of coverage, I could overlook groundbreaking news and just not know it. At the same time, it's good not to oversell it with words like *groundbreaking* when it's really not. It's definitely possible to find good stories in press releases, but because many people get the same announcement, there are limitations and writers don't want to publish the same story as another outlet. By granting embargoes and doing pre-press release briefings, this will ensure that the writer has enough time to put together an insightful piece and get the background information and quotes they need. That additional time is so appreciated.

Hoshaw: Write short, concise emails that get straight to the point. Show how this brand, company, product has real world value. Know the organization you're pitching to and understand and articulate why this story is a good fit for the organization.

Have you ever found a good story via a press release?

Bogo: I have. But more often I find information that supports a story I'm already thinking about and I fold that lead into my other research.

Newman: Yes, but not usually the story that the PR rep is pitching. Reputable info sources I use frequently, often send useful data via press releases, but when they do that I usually go out of my way *not* to write the story right out of the press release. Instead, since I know a lot of my journalistic colleagues are looking at exactly the same info (and some will cover it) I look for side angles or stories within the story. Every now and then I'll even do a debunking story pointing out the lousy info somebody is trying to publicize, with gullible media buying it.

Biggs: No.

Fleming: I have absolutely found my way to good stories via a press release. But the savvy publicist must recognize that the story I want out of your pitch may not be exactly the story you're pitching. The smart publicist will recognize that getting a client mentioned in a piece with a larger context may be just as good as getting a story about that client and nothing else – which might not have happened in the first place.

Thompson: Absolutely. It has to be specific and speak specifically to what I'm interested in. For example, somebody pitched me once to write a story about how economic statistics were broken and a new big data company was trying to solve the problem. I had just been thinking about this issue, so I wrote back and yadda yadda it turned into a story.

Gilbert: All the time! Especially from universities and smaller companies that don't have the bandwidth to send out email blasts or hire a PR firm. Most journalists I know regularly check newswires for new announcements.

What annoys you about press releases?

Hoshaw: My goal is not the same as theirs. I often get pitches that essentially read, "Hey, please promote this company, person, brand, product, etc." My job is not to promote something just because a PR rep says something is cool, interesting, or important – show me why it's cool, interesting, and important and why it's relevant for our audience. Use hyperbole (when possible and if accurate), i.e., "This is the first company to do X, or this product is the biggest X, etc." And understand a publisher's audience. If I write about science for a general audience and you pitch a business story, that's a wasted opportunity to go after the right publication that would be happy to take the pitch.

Newman: The ones targeted at people who cover different beats than I do. The ones sent to me two, three, four times, as if I'll be more likely to respond; sending irrelevant material multiple times doesn't make it any more relevant. Ones that take four paragraphs to get to the point (fat chance I'll read that far). Ones that ask me to "please consider covering" this or that, simply because it happened.

Biggs: They offer no context, no understanding of the receiver, and no story. They are literally the laziest thing a company can do.

Fleming: I receive more than 500 emails a day. An astonishing number of them are pitching topics that neither I nor my staff has ever covered – sent by people who've either never read our publication, or never read our coverage, or noticed what bylines go with what stories.

Thompson: The broad thoughtlessness of many press releases is sort of astonishing. The classic of the genre is putting "Timely Business Story" in the headline. But there are also releases that seem tailored to speak to everybody and appeal to nobody. "Pitch: Better Jobs in America" would be that sort of subject line.

Gilbert: When other journalists get them before me. When there's no contact information for who to reach out to. When key information is left out or left vague.

So the good news is that it's possible to land a good story via press release. But the release must be very well-written, targeted to the right reporter, and sent with a specific story idea in the headline. And you may need some luck and good timing. The bad news is that press releases may not be the right format for most reporters, and sometimes, as Rick Newman noted, you won't get the article you envisioned.

Pitch Letters

A pitch is a brief letter written to a reporter to get them interested in your story. So when you want to reach a particular reporter at a specific publication, write a pitch letter. Whereas press releases reach a wide audience, pitch letters are targeted. Pitches are more specific and informal. Don't write "because we are opening a new hamburger stand and my boss told me to get us on the front page of the local newspaper." That's your goal, not the reporter's.

Figure 1.5 is an example of how not to write a pitch letter. If you have written a pitch letter like this, please consider a career in forensic accounting. Pitches are key components of the public relations strategy. And because they're informal, they're more likely to attract the interest of reporters whose time is precious. A bad pitch will quickly be ignored and earn you a permanent place in the spam folder.

Pitch letters should avoid clichés, notes offering an "exclusive" opportunity, and reminders of talking points (underlining and bolding information) implying that reporters aren't smart enough to figure it out.

Mashable lists its PR Pet Peeves, which include USING ALL CAPS in the subject line, misspelling the names of reporters, and pitching old news. "Sending us an old press release is a lose-lose. For starters, if we research it and see it has been covered a dozen times elsewhere, we probably won't cover it. Additionally, if we research it and

Example of A Flawed Pitch Letter

Generic lead. Never use exclamation points.

Dear Reporter:

Have I got a great column for you!

Pompous, unsubstantiated adjectives.

It's a phenomenal, delightful story about promoting our CEO or President, a leader in his field, who represents the leading, best, top, unique product or service unlike anyone else.

Self-serving. Who cares?

Overused clichés.

You should invite the media to lunch for an EXCLUSIVE interview to discover his award-winning and market-best secrets of leadership and sales success. He might even discuss his unusual talents outside the boardroom, including his passion for golf and his sweater collection. Look us up on the web. What time should we schedule your lunch? I'm sure you will enjoy this **fascinating** opportunity!

Never use caps. Exclusive to whom?

Bragging, not provable.

Boring. Who cares?

Presumptuous. Lunch without a story wastes everyone's time.

Where's the URL?

Never underline and bold.

Figure 1.5. This flawed pitch letter is filled with mistakes commonly made by beginners or nonprofessionals such as small business owners.

see it hasn't been covered anywhere, it makes us question if maybe the story just wasn't newsworthy in the first place." Sending an invite from a smart phone app is also not recommended.

Some Tips on Writing Good Pitch Letters

We all get pitched every day via email to attend events, join charities, buy products, donate to our colleges, and more. What makes *you* respond? Now apply those principles to your queries to the media.

Offer some new and interesting information that makes the reporter look good. Former *Forbes* editor Brett Nelson notes that "solving someone's problem" is his #1 tip to PR professionals for using pitches effectively. "Good articles inform and entertain. The best also solve readers' problems – typically by way of tangible examples showing how, say, a company navigated a partnership with a larger firm, or finagled creative financing in a tight credit market, or turbocharged its growth by building a strong management team."

Nelson's #2 tip advises nailing down the news peg (news angle). "Did you just roll out a new product? Reach an impressive sales milestone? Expand your staff by 50 percent in three months? Reap the benefit of a recent policy change? Again, the examples are myriad. A news peg without an engaging tale or business lesson is a press release. If that's all you have or bothered to come up with, don't bother calling."

The Bad Pitch Blogspot offers a few cringe-worthy examples of horrible pitches along with some solid advice, such as the importance of a dynamite lead: "In that first sentence give the reporter something that will make him say either 'Gee I never knew' or 'That's a fantastic freaking angle for a story.' Or better yet, get him to say both and you win a prize! Don't mess around with formalities. And don't bury the lead, or your angle, in hype, jargon, or buzzwords. Buzzwords are so 1999."

Be familiar with each reporter you try to contact. By reading the stories they've posted and by studying their biography online, you can become familiar with what they need. You might use subtle flattery in your short note ("I noticed your recent story on X, here's something that may be of similar interest . . .") – it can't hurt.

It's crucial that your pitch have a good subject line. Here are two examples where creative subject lines led to major stories:

- When we pitched a story for a former client, Cornell University, our task was to promote a sustainability project in India – a PhD student working with a major chemical company to introduce soybeans to the local diet. Seems dry. But where do you grow soybeans in the slums of India? On the roofs. Which led to the pitch that attracted the reporter, which resulted in this story in the Wall Street Journal: "In India, How Do Rooftop Gardens Grow?"

- For a law firm client, we pitched a young real estate attorney for a major "rising stars" list. These honors are extremely competitive, so the challenge is to make your client shine. In a sea of emails how did we sparkle? We emphasized not just the list of deals but the total amount of money involved. So the headline "Billion Dollar Dealmaker" turned into a successful pitch, a good story, and the cover of the magazine, which also called our client "The Billion Dollar Dealmaker."

To summarize, if you have something interesting to say – with real news value –do your research, make your story compelling, write it to serve the reporter's needs, and be sure to spell everything correctly. That way you'll significantly increase your chances of landing your story. And by eliminating all caps, boldface, and underlining in your pitch, you'll give your wrist a break, too.

Best Words to Use in Pitches

Fractl is a full-service digital marketing agency that specializes in content marketing, social media, and lead generation, with a strong focus on viral marketing as it relates to SEO, rankings, and online growth. The firm published valuable research on the best-performing words used in subject headlines.

Brand Relationship Strategist Andrea Lehr says the research was "based on an analysis of 26,000 pitches pulled from our outreach management software, BuzzStream; no traditional press releases were included. The pitches covered a variety of topics (i.e., both client-facing projects and our own research). Success was determined by whether or not an editor responded to a pitch." Figure 1.6 shows the results of that research.

While some words and phrases were winners, the Fractl group advises PR pros that many terms, including *interactive* and *data,* were deemed to be too common and overused. Figure 1.7 shows which words are overused.

Editorials

Whether it's called an opinion-editorial, content marketing, or something else, a column written by you or your client offering an opinion on a topical issue is an excellent vehicle to establish credibility and raise visibility.

Top 15 Highest-Performing Subject-Line Words

Based on Response Rate

Keyword	Success Percentage for Subject Lines Including the Keyword
Content	30.6%
Size	27.6%
Marketing	24.8%
Know	23.5%
Ideal	23.2%
U.K.	22.6%
Air	19.1%
Image	18.9%
House	18.1%
Travelers	17.8%
Generations	17.8%
Chart	17.8%
Body	17.5%
Show	17.4%
Changed	17.4%

How Does Content Go Viral? 345 Campaigns Reveal 4 Key Factors

Shocking Facts You Probably Don't Know About Body Image

Every Single Incarnation of the USS Enterprise in One Chart

Does Size Really Matter? (For Smartphones, That Is?)

Sci-Fi Project: U.K. to NYC in 37 Minutes? Easy for Tony Stark

Terrifying I-95 Footage Shows 200 Distracted South Florida Drivers in 20 Minutes

Figure 1.6. Top fifteen highest-performing subject-line words, including several examples of the words in use in subject lines. Research by Fractl.

Top 5 Overused Words* in Subject Lines
Based on Response Rate

Keyword	Success Percentage for Subject Lines Including the Keyword
Interactive	9.3%
State	9.9%
U.S.	10.0%
Data	10.3%
Video	10.5%

Figure 1.7. Top five overused words in subject lines. *Overused words refers to words that are used in at least 500 subject lines that have the lowest success rates. Research by Fractl.

As the *New York Times* states, "The name 'op-ed' is derived from 'opposite the editorial page.' The op-ed pages feature opinion pieces written by outside contributors and *The Times's* own team of columnists. . . . Editorials are written by individual *New York Times* editorial board members in consultation with their colleagues and editors and reflect the opinions of the diverse, 16-member *Times* editorial board." In other words, an op-ed features the opinion of someone outside the publication, and that could be you or your client.

An op-ed is much more prestigious than a letter to the editor, which comes in response to something already written. Whenever possible you want to be proactive and contribute your own op-ed rather than respond to someone else's with a letter to the editor, which is reactive. The National Recreational Park Association (of all places) produced a great summary on how to write an op-ed that advises writers to "strengthen your message by citing national trends that show support for your issue . . . localize the story . . . and highlight the success of congressional support for the issue."

Some Tips for Writing Good Editorials

You shouldn't view op-eds as advertisements. They're not for trumpeting your product as a solution. They're a more subtle form of publicity, for showing that you or your client are knowledgeable about the subject and have something important to say about it. Here are tips from seasoned media professionals on writing op-eds:

- **Be sharp.** "Before making a point, you have to have a point," says David Whitley, a sports columnist for *The Orlando Sentinel.* "A good way to find one is to write the headline before writing the column. Even if you don't have to write your own headlines, do it in your head. This will sharpen the focus on what you want readers to take away."

- **Be opinionated.** Hence the "op" half of op-ed. "I want an opinion, not a 'how-to' or an 'explainer,' says Charles Crumpley, the editor of the *Los Angeles Business Journal.* "A lot of times I get product or service pitches that are packaged as an op-ed. Lawyers send stories about a new law and they ask you to call them at the end of the article. For the most part, those get rejected."

- **Be controversial.** Adrienne Selko, who manages the editorial content for *IndustryWeek.com,* invites provocative prose – as long as the assertions are well argued. "Headlines pull readers in," says Selko. "I welcome submissions that are somewhat controversial."

- **Be helpful.** Grousing without resolution (or at least a general road map) won't get you very far, either. "Readers like action steps about what can be done," says Selko. "Offer a solution of some kind."

Figure 1.8 shows an example of well written editorial.

It's also important to consider the following before you begin to write your editorial:

- **The Publication.** Are they conservative? Liberal? Rock and roll? Arts? Features-based? Tied to the 24-7 news cycle? Remember the old saying, "Bait the hook to suit the fish." Find publications that will be receptive to your editorial.

- **Timeliness.** If you or your client want to comment on a presidential debate, a plane crash, a stock market move, or something similar, don't send an editorial three days after the event. Most media want analysis and opinion as quickly as possible.

- **Expertise.** Offer a unique perspective based on experience that no one else possesses. Every news outlet has journalists on staff and several freelancers. What unusual and relevant opinions can you offer?

Rules for Saving Your Story

It's always a good idea to be flexible. Sometimes ideas and pitches don't work at first. When that happens, adjust. Here are my rules for saving your story:

Think Local. The job of local papers is to write about local people and businesses. Any ties you can make to the hometown community greatly increase the chances of success. Even when national stories break, editors and reporters always search for the local angle. Make their jobs easier for feature stories by inserting a person with local ties or a business that operates in the local area.

Think Trade Press. The job of the trade press is to accurately report on and, in many cases, promote the specific industry they cover. There are hundreds, if not thousands, of magazines, blogs, websites, and even some cable channels devoted to gem stones, public speaking, bathroom fixtures, spirituality, yoga, hospitality, carpets, etc. They need good stories.

Meet Alumni Reporters. If you're a university, law firm, major company, small business owner, entrepreneur, publicist, or anyone else who needs publicity, it's always a good idea to make friends with journalists. Did they go to your college? Work at your firm? Do you have contacts in common? Connect with them on that level, make friends, then pitch them your story.

Figure 1.8. Example of a good editorial.

- **Trends.** Nobody wants a sales pitch about your product. Inform the audience about what you or your company are doing to illuminate a bigger issue or trend that affects the general public.

There are several ways reporters find stories. Breaking news, personal connections, responding to pitches, even discovering them by chance. And reporters are increasingly using social media to find stories. The next chapter will investigate what works for publicists and what doesn't in using social media to reach reporters.

CHAPTER 2

Social Media

Lloyd Christmas: *What are my chances*
Mary Swanson: *Not good.*
Lloyd: *You mean, not good like one out of a hundred?*
Mary: *I'd say more like one out of a million.*
(long pause)
Lloyd: *So, you're telling me there's a chance.*
YEAH!

— From *Dumb and Dumber*

THERE'S A FAMOUS SCENE in the movie *Dumb and Dumber* where goofball limousine driver Lloyd Christmas, played by Jim Carrey, asks his crush, beautiful Mary Swanson (Lauren Holly) if she could ever love him. The way she rebuffs him mirrors the world of social media. Yes, there's a chance an unknown can succeed, becoming influential, famous, and wealthy. But it's a very slim possibility.

Actually, it's microscopic. But like Lloyd Christmas, most social media users buy into the myth of quick, powerful, viral media success.

Look at the names of some of these books: *Social Media Made Me Rich*, *How to Skyrocket Your Business Through Social Media Marketing!*, *Social Media: Master, Manipulate, and Dominate Social Media Marketing*, and *The Art of Social Media: Power Tips for Power Users*. If social media was magical, and anyone could do it, why doesn't everyone have 100,000 Twitter followers? Why aren't they LinkedIn Influencers? Why don't they get 10,000 comments every time they post on Facebook? Why aren't they endlessly retweeted and paid for every thought? Why aren't they rich and famous?

Yes, Lloyd Christmas, social media can be effective for public relations – in moderation.

Every day, corporations, PR agencies, non-profits, and individuals post text, audio, video, and other content that inform their audiences, connect with influencers, and update their information for the general public. Most of these duties produce daily incremental benefits. Much of the time, modest goals can be achieved. So social media can be effective – as long as your goals are modest. And despite bashing the social media hype in the first part of this chapter, we will show you the most effective social media strategies later on.

In baseball terms, these efforts produce bunt singles, an occasional double, but most of the time you're just sitting on the bench with teammates, talking to the usual group of friends and colleagues. And that's OK. Social media makes some PR functions more efficient.

But the goal of attaining magical success, with little effort, is not realistic. How many PR firms offer to "create a video that goes viral" as part of their service offerings? Many of them do, but it's misleading marketing.

Social media success is difficult. It can take weeks, months, or years to build an audience. Waiting for easy riches and quick results is like counting on a $100 million Powerball ticket to pay off the mortgage, send your kids to college, and buy matching Lamborghinis for you and your spouse.

Here are four major myths about social media that most authors, publishers, and conferences charging $5,000 don't want you to know about.

The Four Major Social Media Fallacies

Major Fallacy #1: Opinions are special.
Fact: Social media is very common.

The days of easy social media success are long gone.

The only person with a Morse code machine in the Old West heard the news faster than anyone else. The first family on the block with a color TV set was very popular. The first couple to "accidentally" release a sex tape became notorious. The first dozen people on Facebook or Twitter enjoyed a big advantage, building their brands, enforcing their opinions, ensuring that they would be viewed. The next time you get the wrong sandwich at a restaurant, or the airline loses your luggage, try tweeting your displeasure. Good luck getting a response. You'll be lucky if your friends comment. (Figure 2.1)

The Days of Easy Social Media Success Are Long Gone

Monthly Active Users

- Facebook 2.23 billion
- YouTube 1.9 billion
- Instagram 1 billion
- LinkedIn 562 million
- Twitter 335 million
- Snapchat 300 million
- Pinterest 250 million

Daily Postings

- 4.75 billion items of content shared daily on Facebook
- 5 billion videos watched on YouTube every day
- 500 million tweets sent daily on Twitter

Figure 2.1. Facebook statistics from Zephoria, September 2018. Other statistics from Omnicore Agency, September 2018.

Major Fallacy #2: Anyone can be influential.

Fact: Traffic flocks to the famous.

There are a few people who became famous on social media. There are also a few people who are renowned for playing the cello or winning a gold medal in ping pong. It's possible, but not likely. The odds are simply against the average person becoming influential this way. Just like in the real world, corporations and celebrities are the influencers. Brands and celebrities dominate the social media traffic. See for yourself – check out the top ten blogs on the Internet (Figure 2.2) and the top ten Twitter followings (Figure 2.3).

In other words, if you're Katy Perry or LeBron James, and you have millions of followers on social media, social media works well. Your model is one to millions, the

Top 10 Blogs on the Internet

- Huffington Post 110,000,000
- TMZ 30,000,000
- Business Insider 25,5000,000
- Mashable 24,000,000
- Gizmodo 23,500,000
- LifeHacker 23,250,000
- TheVerge 18,000,000
- The Daily Beast 15,500,000
- Tech Crunch 15,000,000
- Perez Hilton 14,500,000

Figure 2.2. Top ten blogs on the Internet based on estimated unique monthly visitors. Source: eBizMBA Rank, updated average of each website's Alex Global Traffic Rank, and U.S. Traffic Rank from Compete and Quantcast, May 2018.

broadcast model, rather than one-to-one-to-one, etc., the sharing or viral method, which is extremely rare. Even worse, when something appears to go viral, it hasn't. According to ChartBeat, most people who like, click, or forward an article barely open it. "Most people who click don't read," says Tony Halle of ChartBeat, a data analytics company. "A stunning 55 percent spent fewer than 15 seconds actively on a page."

Major Fallacy #3: Influencers will help you.
Fact: Influencers are expensive, or impossible, to find.

Author B. J. Mendelson caused a firestorm with the publication of his book, *Social Media is Bullshit*. He noted that influencers, those magical beasts who will catapult your idea or product into the mainstream with a single tweet or post, are as real as mermaids or the Loch Ness monster. "I don't dispute that people with actual influence exist, possessing a voice that can reach the seventh layer of Hell from

Top 10 Twitter Users

- Katy Perry 106,886,460
- Justin Bieber 104,360,967
- Barack Obama 101,923,994
- Rihanna 87,305,512
- Taylor Swift 83,406,174

- Lady Gaga 76,700,672
- Ellen Degeneres 76,235,817
- Cristiano Ronaldo 74,305,413
- YouTube 70,715,020
- Justin Timberlake 64,351,561

Figure 2.3. Top ten Twitter followings based on number of followers. Source: Twitter Counter, August 2018.

the ninth. What I dispute, and I'm not alone . . . is that the people who possess this mysterious ability are easily identifiable using services like Klout, and accessed, celebrities notwithstanding. Don't waste your money trying to find, identify, and influence these influencers."

Even worse, many celebrities purchase millions of fake users from sites like Devumi, falsely inflating their supposed influence. (More on this later in the chapter).

Major Fallacy #4: Anyone can go viral.
Fact: Going viral organically is extremely rare.

Most viral sensations were purchased or promoted.

Nick Westergaard of Brand Driven Digital says many triumphs are probably luck. "The fact is, viral videos – content that spreads like a crazy wildfire across the Internet – are a myth. Or, rather, the act of creating these sensations out of the box is a myth. There isn't any magic dust that marketers can sprinkle over our content to endow it with these powers. The fact is, these phenomena are largely the result of random chance."

Sharad Goel and Ashton Anderson of Stanford University and Jake Hofman and Duncan Watts of Microsoft Research debunked the viral media unicorn in their widely read study in the January 2016 edition of *Management Science*. "We find that structural virality is typically low, and remains so independent of size, suggesting that popularity is largely driven by the size of the largest broadcast," Goel says. The authors note that even with viral growth, 99 percent of the time, the posts are only forwarded once.

Even worse, the chance of something going viral on Twitter? One in a million. Lloyd Christmas would be proud!

The research suggests that information spreads like a telecast of a popular TV show, such as the Super Bowl, instead of a fast-moving virus. Broadcasts distribute directly to people, whereas viral distribution moves from one person to another to another, etc.

L2's *Intelligence Report: Video* finds that the "viral video" is a myth. L2 noted that the supposedly viral "Real Beauty Sketches" ad from Dove, which was called the "most viral ad video of all time" in 2013, obtained about 75 percent of its views via paid advertising.

Social Media – More Challenges

According to a 2014 Gallup survey, social media doesn't always work for large companies with giant budgets. In "The Myth of Social Media," Gallup found that 72 percent of adults use social media often. Most firms employ at least one person, and often a whole team, to increase brand visibility via social media platforms. U.S. firms spent an estimated $5.1 billion on social media advertising in 2013, with a projected growth to almost $15 billion by 2018.

But clearly, Gallup believes this is a waste of money. "Most consumers don't visit to engage with brands – they are there to interact with people they know." According to Gallup research, the vast majority of consumers (94 percent) who use Facebook, Twitter, and other social networking channels do so to connect with family and friends. They are far less interested in learning about companies and/or their products, which implies that many companies have social media strategies in place that may be largely misdirected.

And only five percent of consumers said that social media had a great deal of influence on their purchasing decisions.

The fallacy that users flocking to social media view content supplied by PR specialists or advertisers and happily join the conversation is crazier than a children's movie where a cute Shetland pony wins the Kentucky Derby. Gallup goes on to say, "Consumers are highly adept at tuning out brand-related Facebook and Twitter content. These channels do not motivate prospective customers to consider trying a brand or recommending a brand to others."

Back to Mendelson and *Social Media is Bullshit*. He declares that social media, Web 2.0, and Internet marketing are incredibly overhyped by gullible media and by evangelists who simply promote their own expertise. "When you think about it, social media has all the hallmarks of a get-rich-quick scheme, which fits perfectly with the Great Depression-like conditions many Americans have faced since 2007: You don't need to have any specific kind of skill set to use any of the platforms, and there's little risk involved. And like other get-rich-quick schemes, a few people even got rich, which encouraged more people to participate and buy a shovel."

Mendelson says highly paid speakers, authors, and futurists who claim special digital expertise make millions of dollars spreading their malarkey online, in person, or in print. Like many carnival barkers, preachers, politicians, or other hucksters, their main goal in converting the masses to their cause isn't salvation but profit. "The rhetoric they spew is usually to the effect that people today have the power to do anything without resources, funding, connections, training, education, and so forth. After amassing a large enough audience of willing listeners, they then cash in on the traffic generated from their talk in the form of advertisements, speaking fees, and book deals."

In a 2016 interview with me, Mendelson expanded upon the pack mentality regarding the effectiveness of social media, due mostly to books and personal appearances by these futurists. "People listen to successful people," he said. "We're busy. So, there aren't many of us who are going to go digging into these people to see if their story holds up to any scrutiny. They totally should, but they don't. If the media tells you these idiots are geniuses at marketing and business, you're not going to question it. And that's the world we live in. Nobody looks too deeply into anything anymore, so if you're a con artist, there's never been a better time than right now to fake your way to the top."

Sometimes the news consumed on social media has very little credibility. According to a study released by the Pew Research Center in 2016: "Social media, on the other hand, is trusted by a slim minority – only 4 percent of web-using adults have a lot of trust in the information they find on social media. And that rises to only 7 percent among those who get news on these sites."

Unfortunately, when social media works, it often acts as an accelerator for fake news, like tons of organic fertilizer on a field of corn.

A great example comes from reporter Sapna Maheshwari of the *New York Times*. In her November 2016 story, "How Fake News Goes Viral: A Case Study," she notes how a conservative voter took a photo of buses driving through Austin, Texas, during the presidential campaign season. Without any evidence, he labeled the passengers as paid protesters sent to heckle candidate Donald Trump by the Clinton campaign.

This was a lie. But the tweet was nevertheless copied, pasted, and shared more than 350,000 times on Facebook. It was then picked up by the conservative media and right-wing blogs, each quoting the other as "news sources," and amplified like an echo chamber.

This phenomenon has happened several times, including false stories such as "Pizzagate," about a fake child trafficking ring operating out of the basement of a restaurant in Washington, DC. The story was easily debunked. There was no trafficking ring and no basement either. But the story grew in importance once it leaped from social media onto Fox News, Breitbart News, InfoWars, and other right-wing media.

So, does this prove that anyone can create fake news and make it work? Not exactly.

Take the phenomenon of Russia's efforts to sow discord among the American electorate in 2016 and persuade voters to sympathize with Republican candidate Trump. This type of campaign is very rare and very expensive. It required millions of dollars, a few months if not years of planning, hundreds of full-time technology experts posting 24 hours a day, and, in the end, some luck.

Business Insider summarized the Russian campaign:

- They created Facebook events for rallies in several states. Russia-linked Facebook groups like Heart of Texas and SecuredBorders tried to organize anti-immigrant rallies in Texas and Idaho in the months leading up to the election. Another group, Being Patriotic, organized pro-Donald Trump flash mobs across Florida in August 2016, according to *The Daily Beast*.

- They purchased ads that promoted outsider candidates and exploited racial tensions. The ads boosted Trump, Green Party candidate Jill Stein, and Democratic candidate Bernie Sanders, and at least one ad centered on the Black Lives Matter movement. A group impersonating a California-based Muslim organization was also set up to push fake stories about Hillary Clinton, the Democratic nominee.

- They created accounts to amplify emails stolen from the Democratic National Committee. Members of the hacking group connected to the GRU created the DCLeaks and Guccifer 2.0 accounts in June 2016 to help spread the emails stolen in late 2015, *The Washington Post* reported.

Not everyone can perform such expensive, detailed campaigns. And without the quirks of the Electoral College or the last-minute James Comey memo reopening the investigation into Clinton's emails, this fake news campaign might have failed.

Social Media – The Good

The Gold Rush is over, but there is public relations value to be gained by using social media. The biggest challenge is first to understand the social media process, create realistic goals, then swing for singles and doubles without expecting grand slams every time at bat.

Here's the straight talk about social media and public relations. Obviously, the internet transformed the media forever. It altered the news delivery system, zapped our eyeballs with radiation, and ushered audiences from print to online to social media on screens, tablets, and phones.

Without the internet, there would be no instant news available on smart phones around the world, we wouldn't know the exact locations of reality TV stars every minute, and we wouldn't see the opinions of our many friends, enemies, and strangers via tweets, message boards, snaps, and posts.

But the biggest change affects breaking news. Instead of waiting for the morning newspaper, evening news, or weekly magazine, citizens can view stories in real time. Plus, opinions and comments appear much more frequently and instantaneously within the news websites and online in social media outlets.

What does this mean for small businesses, individuals, and publicists?

There are some limitations. Most importantly, social media is not usually as effective as traditional PR methods

Social Media for Public Relations

Works For	Fails For
Crisis PR	Generating story leads
Research on products	Reaching influencers
Finding reporters	Contacting reporters
Creating groups	Going "viral"
Reacting to customers or critics	Pitching feature stories

Figure 2.4. What works and doesn't work using social media for public relations.

(more on that in the chapter on PR measurement). Figure 2.4 shows where social media works and doesn't work for public relations.

Out of the millions or billions who have tried, a few social media superstars have cracked the secret code. Figure 2.5 shows an analysis of *Time* magazine's lists of the most influential people on the internet from 2015, 2016, and 2017. Over those three years there were 71 people listed, but some people were listed two or three times. The magazine "sized up contenders by looking at their global impact on social media and their overall ability to drive news."

The best chance for success, according to *Time*, is to be a singer/dancer/comedian/actor, followed distantly by political commentators, then journalists.

For the group as a whole, Twitter is the most popular platform, followed by Youtube and Instagram. Most of the top influencers are in the entertainment industry (31), followed by politics (12). Far behind are journalists/authors, fitness/sports figures, fashionistas, and others.

Here's a quick equation; let's call it Rob's Stratagem for Social Media Success. It's still extremely rare to vault from anonymity to become a Social Media Superstar, but those who succeeded followed COP.

Massive consistent **Content**

Original opinions and news

the right **Platform**

Singers and comedians do best on YouTube, where videos showcase their talents and appearance; fashion designers and photographers score highest on Instagram and Pinterest to highlight their visual appeal; and journalists, bloggers, and activists utilize Twitter to post their news and insights. A note about "massive consistent content." Activists for Black Lives Matter became influential by chronicling, posting, and commenting on the movement with daily, hourly, and sometimes more frequent updates.

It wasn't easy, and it didn't happen instantly. Once the protests ended, the influence of political commenters waned. That's why consistency and relevance are so important.

How Social Media Has Changed Public Relations

Public relations had to evolve in order to survive. The biggest changes in public relations include revolutions in:

Most Influential People on the Internet
(categorized by type)

- Professionals (famous before the Internet): 28
- Amateurs (not famous before social media): 43

TOTAL: 71

Industry of Influencers

- Entertainment: 31
- Politics: 12
- Journalism/Author: 5
- Fitness/Sports: 5
- Graphics/Photographer: 4
- Other (Non-Fashion): 7
- Other (Fashion): 4
- Teen: 3

TOTAL: 71

Primary Social Media Platform
Used by Influencers

- Twitter: 23
- Instagram: 15
- YouTube: 15
- Facebook: 5
- Snapchat: 1
- Other: 12

TOTAL: 71

Influencers Top Three Industries with
Primary Platform Used

Entertainment: 31 (Amateurs: Youtube; Professionals: Instagram)

Politics: 12 (Twitter)

Journalists & Authors: 5 (Twitter)

Figure 2.5. Summary analysis of *Time* magazine's lists of social media influencers from 2015, 2016, and 2017.

- **Conversations.** The old top-down model of PR, where publicists need to reach reporters to create a story in the media, still exists, but it's no longer the exclusive path to media placement. In theory, anyone can bypass journalists to address an audience. All-Pro wide receiver Antonio Brown of the Pittsburgh Steelers and actor Gwyneth Paltrow don't need megaphones – their audiences are waiting to read their posts. But since anyone can post, and almost everyone does, most posts are ignored – they're each just one of billions. When stories do reach the mainstream press (most often through traditional PR methods), however, social media can serve as a great amplifier – many people share the stories and add comments as well, generating ongoing conversations and publicity.

- **Crisis media.** For crisis public relations, when there's an accident, plane crash, product recall, scandal, or similar event, social media can be very effective. The speed and direct communication work best to inform consumers affected by the crisis in real time. PR is faster and often more powerful when it's online – for good or bad, depending on your perspective. The viral video of stand-up comic Hannibal Buress joking about Bill Cosby and sexual assault created so much bad publicity that Cosby's reputation was destroyed. The lesson: PR pros must monitor social media platforms and respond to crises in seconds or minutes rather than hours.

- **Research.** Social media is a real benefit to publicists and communications professionals (not so much for reporters who are trying to hide from publicists). It's made it much easier to find reporters, producers, and editors via their own websites or by using search engines and paid services such as Cision and Meltwater. But the new technologies can be overrated. PR professionals still need to use traditional PR tactics to engage with these media people. Unless you have old school talents such as writing, charm, great contacts, and/or incredibly interesting clients, tweeting from your Apple iPhone 10 to your buddies in Austin and West Hollywood while sipping lattes in Brooklyn won't get you an office on Park Avenue or Sunset Boulevard.

How the Internet Hasn't Changed Public Relations

- **You still need a story.** Cute cat videos and trendy porkpie hats are fabulous for getting attention. Post that stuff and you'll get tons of likes, but you won't convince anyone about anything. Good publicists do two things extremely well – they sift through all the story possibilities like a miner looking for the platinum vein and then communicate the value of the gem in as few words as possible to the right audience.

- **You must be able to write well.** There are millions of blogs. If you write a blog in the wilderness and no one reads it, does it make an impact? Blogs and posts are as common as reality-TV stars, and just as worthless. And most are poorly written. Have a point. Get to the point.

- **You need contacts.** Forget Twitter followers and Facebook friends. You need influencers. Nine out of ten times, that means reporters. Brad Pitt or Sheryl Sandberg aren't wearing your clients' jeans or sunglasses or representing your charity and taking photos with your client because you met them at a party and had a good vibe. Sometimes a great story or great writing (see above) can net you a fantastic article in the media, but it never hurts to meet reporters in person at networking events. Journalists get up to 1,000 emails per day; what's going to make them open yours? PR professionals, small business owners, entrepreneurs, and students will find that attending conferences, lunches, seminars, and similar meetings to greet journalists in person is a much better use of their time than days and weeks on social media.

- **You need a good client or cause.** Every PR firm or internal PR professional loves their clients. Our clients are the best of the best, of course. But sometimes a client may not have a compelling story or may be on the defensive, which makes your job much more difficult (but that's why crisis PR pays so well).

- **You need people skills.** Enthusiasm, kindness, respect, and knowing how to pitch and respond in a professional manner will never go out of style.

How to Get the Most Out of Social Media

Using social media for public relations can be difficult. It's very competitive. But somewhere in the vast wasteland, PR professionals, small business owners, and entrepreneurs can find useful tools for harnessing the web (Figure 2.6).

Rule One: Be Brief – Don't Be Boring

Greg Galant is the CEO of Muck Rack, a website that connects PR practitioners to journalists via free and paid resources and champions exciting and meaningful posts.

Boring doesn't work on social media. The last thing you want to do is simply take a press release and post it to a social network. It's much better to tailor your announcement in a human way for each social network your audience will care about. On Twitter, come up with an exciting way to say your announcement in 117 characters (remember you'll need to save 23 characters for your link). [Now that would be 257 characters, since Twitter raised their limit to 280 characters in 2017.] Find a great image related to your announcement to include in your posts to Instagram and Pinterest. Make a video about your announcement for YouTube. Even on social networks where you can post a lot of text, like Facebook and Tumblr, don't post a press release. Rewrite it without the jargon, stock quotes, and meaningless phrases (e.g., 'we're thrilled to announce' or 'best in class') as though you're telling a friend why your announcement matters.

Jeet Banerjee, an entrepreneur, speaker, and author, swears by one service to promote his upcoming speeches – Instagram. Keeping the information meaningful is key to his success. "I've found the greatest conversions/success through promoting on Instagram," Banerjee says. "Since speeches are such a visual thing, by posting promo pictures or pictures after my event, I get the highest amount of conversions and responses. I have constantly used Instagram more as a running picture blog to showcase who I am and what exciting things I'm working on next. This is much easier on the eyes and far more appealing to the press."

Rule Two: Be Newsworthy

In the old days, pre-social media, when a news story broke, PR pros would send emails and faxes and make phone calls to their lists of reporters to announce that their client was available to comment on the story right away.

Now, for breaking news, journalists need an expert to comment on a situation quickly, in real time, via a phone interview, video-conference, live video interview, tweet, email, instant message, or other method. Reporters generally contact their usual list of suspects, experts whom they know and trust.

Smart PR pros, small business owners, and entrepreneurs can sometimes insert themselves or their clients into a story. Here's an example of "insertion," which has been around since Ivey Lee and Edward Bernays engaged in PR.

Sometimes a story falls from the sky. When actor Harrison Ford crashed his classic airplane on a golf course in Venice, California, the media needed experts. All the public knew, at first, was: Famous Actor. Plane Crash. Then it became apparent that Ford was flying a World War II vintage plane. If you were an expert on planes, or had a client in the aviation industry, this was your chance. An opportunistic publicist or entrepreneur would call the media, give them

Six Rules for Using Social Media for PR

Be Brief – Don't Be Boring

Be Newsworthy

Be Consistent – Post Lots of Quality Content

Be Helpful

Use Facebook Groups

Be Live – Use VIdeo if Possible

Figure 2.6. Follow these six rules to get the most out of social media.

information about the plane, when it was built, its safety record, how many are still in operation, and other data.

Insertion can be used for almost any breaking news story every day: Black Lives Matter protest. Police shooting. Police being shot. Terrorist attack. Super Bowl. Stock market falls sharply. Stock market rebounds sharply. Government officials deny dangerous amounts of lead in the drinking water. New study shows officials lied about amounts of lead in the drinking water.

The model remains the same – pay attention to a breaking news story. If you're an expert or your client is an expert, prepare an opinion on the story. (It's also smart to have a short biography prepared in advance, and make sure that the bio is on your website and Twitter page.) Contact reporters and producers who are covering the story. On Twitter, follow the hashtags.

Rule Three: Be Consistent – Post Lots of Quality Content

Look at the amateur celebrities who have built huge followings. They post videos, photos, and tweets with machinelike regularity. New information and new content constantly entertain their audiences. Like a TV program, magazine, or newspaper, there must be a reason for followers to return.

Let's look at some examples:

- Sex educator Laci Green on YouTube has almost 1.5 million followers. There are several hundred videos posted with links to her media appearances (yet even more content) with new episodes posted weekly.

- Fitness trainer Kayla Itsines created the "Fitspiration" profile with digital workouts and nutrition guides on Instagram, and constant photos and postings allow her to attract 8.8 million followers.

- Journalists and social activists increase their audiences and influence with live tweeting and consistent social media activity by following and reporting on breaking news.

Rule Four: Be Helpful

Ayelet Noff, the CEO of digital public relations company Blonde 2.0, makes friends with the media via social networking. Instead of contacting them by way of Facebook or Twitter with a note ("Have I got a great story for you!") that's destined to send all your PR efforts to purgatory and your email to the blocked address list, Noff preaches payoffs instead of pestering. "A great way to get your story covered is to be on the giving end instead of the receiving end with press. Too often we only try to 'get a story' from a reporter, instead of thinking what could be useful/helpful to this writer."

Noff works with a startup that helps passengers get compensation from airlines when their flights are delayed or canceled. "We continuously search for reporters who are going to be at major conferences (CES, SXSW, etc.) and are experiencing flight issues, and tweet them, letting them know about the service and how we can help them get compensated. By doing so, we are not only making the reporters aware of our service, but we also help them out at a time of real need."

Rule Five: Use Facebook Groups

There's a PR person in Orange County whom I used to follow. Her posts included "I'm at the gym!" and "I'm going on a hike, feel the burn!" along with photos of friends at parties.

Then it hit me. Facebook is a lot like Orange County: shallow, narcissistic, digitally and/or surgically enhanced, but mostly harmless. These posts might drive business for party planning or fashion or cosmetics, but for the rest of us who work in academia or engineering, science, legal, or other industries, Facebook is usually not helpful.

Your posts and information shouldn't be in the same newsfeed as wacky animals, political rants, and vacation photos of sunburned partyers with bad tattoos. There are some exceptions, such as using Facebook for community outreach, building groups, and certain brand promotion, but there are more effective tools in the social media arsenal.

"Facebook is bad for business," says B. J. Mendelson. "Either it's a total waste of funds or the results are nowhere near worth the amount of time, energy, and effort placed to get them. Facebook is specifically built for friends and family. If you want to share pictures with mom, awesome! For small business, money spent on social media is money wasted."

PR blogger Jeremy Porter recommends some uses. "Facebook Groups are an excellent way to manage membership relationships for a group or organization. If you're just starting a group or looking for a more cost-effective tool for managing communications to your members, posting an events calendar, or providing additional networking benefits for your members, Facebook Groups is an excellent option – and it falls in the 'PR' category."

Rule Six: Be Live – Use Video if Possible

During a crisis, when possible, you or someone from your PR team should respond quickly and directly to media coverage. Monitor your business on social media and respond to tweets, mentions, and comments on your company's profiles in a timely manner. Social media is real-time, so the faster you respond, the better your customer service will look.

If possible, suggest that customers contact you privately to send their email addresses or phone numbers for more in-depth discussion. On Twitter you must follow your customer, so she can send a direct message to you. On Facebook fan pages you must share a personal profile that the customer can send a message to.

The American Express Small Business Forum advises companies: "Sometimes bad things happen to good companies. Websites crash. C-level executives are indicted. Facilities burn down or flood. When crises arise, you need a

PR response team in place to take charge and deal directly with media, providing up-to-the minute support that reassures the public and customers. Some of the worst crisis PR in recent months occurred when companies defaulted to Twitter to handle press inquiries. Media went berserk and wrote about their frustration in trying to find a live human to answer questions. Angry customers used companies' own tweets against them – retweeting the posts with 'boos' added."

The *Social Media Examiner* offers some examples of crisis management and the social media tactics that work for various situations. "Social media is public. Your fans and followers have the right to make negative comments – it's your company's job to turn those negative comments around and defend yourself to change it from a negative to a positive situation."

YouTube can work very well. Some channels, particularly tech-savvy ones such as *Forbes, Gizmodo, Tech Crunch, Yahoo Tech*, and *Engadget*, post videos they receive from third parties if they're appropriate and professionally presented. A few reasons for using YouTube videos include kicking off a campaign, responding to a crisis, or trying to extend your brand.

Mashable recommends that you leverage YouTube and other video-sharing sites by sharing your videos with reporters and bloggers. "To be truly successful, online videos must be developed with the web viewer in mind, and they must add value to the conversation. If your videos aren't high-quality, then your emails to bloggers and reporters will be just another piece of junk mail."

Twitter is the Best

If you have to choose one platform for social media, many industries choose Twitter. It appears to be the best platform for public relations.

The Muck Rack website follows trending stories in the news via Twitter. Their community features thousands of PR professionals and journalists. They conducted a survey of several hundred journalists about social media and PR. The results were conclusive:

What social network is most valuable professionally?
- Twitter: 80%
- Facebook: 13%
- LinkedIn: 4%
- Other: 3%

Do you like it when PR pros follow you on social media?
- Like: 86%
- Don't like: 14%

How do you prefer to be pitched?
- Email: 93%
- Phone: 3%
- Twitter: 2%
- Other: 2%

Twitter isn't easy. Like a marriage, a topspin backhand in tennis, or the last season of "Mr. Robot," it takes time and effort, and there's some frustration involved. But it's definitely worth it.

Here's an example from a very small startup. Let's say you're a college student. You and your brother sell vintage T-shirts purchased at garage sales and thrift stores. The T-shirts are posted on Instagram. These are the steps you should take to generate public relations coverage:

- Target media where you'd like to be seen – *Wall Street Journal, CNN, Buzzfeed, Rolling Stone*, etc.

- Find reporters who cover similar businesses or topics. In this example, it would be vintage clothing, classic rock, old school hip-hop, etc.

- Friend or link to these reporters on Twitter and Instagram.

- Write them an email. Reference their previous stories, genuinely compliment the stories you liked. Let them know about your business. Send your Twitter, Instagram, and other handles where your T-shirts can be seen. Briefly announce your story: How do two college students pay off their student debt and have fun at the same time?

- If a reporter responds, follow up and give them more information. Bonus advice: Start with your school paper – that way the national media and trade media can see what the story looks like. They won't consider your college paper a competitor.

Public relations can be like matchmaking. You're trying to connect and amplify yourself, your client, or your story to a wider, mass audience via traditional or social media. For PR professionals, small business owners, and entrepreneurs, there are three main uses for Twitter:

- **Announcements.** You want to tell the public something about you, your business, or your client – such as a new product, an award, an upcoming event, or an introduction into a new market – or you want to keep your audience updated during a crisis or emergency.

- **Research.** You want to find out what competitors, clients, friends, media, or influencers are tweeting about.

- **Networking.** You want to meet new influencers, clients, friends, competitors, or reporters and follow them and get them to follow you.

Twitter sometimes allows publicists and business people to send direct messages to journalists. If you follow a reporter, sometimes that reporter will follow you back. If the journalist chooses to allow direct messages, you can contact them that way. Most reporters don't (for obvious reasons), but if they do, it can be an excellent shortcut to communicate with them.

Here's a guide to what you need to know about Twitter and public relations, starting with the basics.

What is Twitter?

"Facebook is like a party in your backyard," says author Andreas Ramos in his book, #TwitterBook: *How to Really Use Twitter*. "You invite 100 friends and family. When you talk, only those around you can hear you, not the entire party, not the neighborhood, not the city. You can't post a message that can be seen by the one billion people on Facebook. And when you post on Facebook to your friends,

Facebook won't show your message to all of your friends. It shows the message to only about 15 percent of your friends. Twitter is like the Egyptian revolution. Everyone mills around in chaos. Everything goes out to everyone on all sides: friends, enemies, demonstrators, the government, the army, journalists, and the rest of the world."

Unlike Facebook, Twitter restricts users to 280 characters for each tweet so there's a premium on short, punchy writing rather than extended rants. In late 2017 Twitter doubled the character limit from 140 to 280. In a blog post titled "Giving You More Characters to Express Yourself," Twitter product manager Aliza Rosen noted, "When I tweet in English, I quickly run into the 140-character limit and have to edit my tweet so it fits. Sometimes, I have to remove a word that conveys an important meaning or emotion, or I don't send my tweet at all. But when Iku tweets in Japanese, he doesn't have the same problem. He finishes sharing his thought and still has room to spare. This is because in languages like Japanese, Korean, and Chinese you can convey about double the amount of information in one character as you can in many other languages, such as English, Spanish, Portuguese, or French. We want every person around the world to easily express themselves on Twitter, so we're doing something new: we're going to try out a longer limit, 280 characters, in languages impacted by cramming (which is all except Japanese, Chinese, and Korean).

How Do I Start?

Max Benavidez, a former official at Claremont McKenna College and former journalist, advises users, "Start by setting up a test account, spend time on the network seeing how people in your field and related fields use it. In particular, look at how journalists and key bloggers in your field use it. Wait to make a pitch until you are comfortable using it. Start with subtle engagement."

Grant Marek, Senior Editor for Chubbies Shorts, a trendy site for men in their 20s, told the website Muck Rack that he recommends searching by hashtag, known as hashtag crawling. "If you aren't including hashtags in your tweets, you're doing something wrong. I follow over 2,000 people, which means I only see snippets of what those people are saying in my feed on any given day, but when it comes to hashtags that matter to us, I scroll through *all of them,* whether it's #sfmuni or #bart or #burningman or #saas (software as a service)."

How Do I Get Followers?

The website Twiends, which bills itself as a "leading directory of social media users," offers some tips to boost your audience.

- **Run a contest:** Offer a good prize and make sure you clearly communicate the rules of entry. If your prize is related to your brand, then it can also help find targeted followers who are interested in your area of expertise.

- **Join a directory:** There are dozens of directories of Twitter users online, including Twiends, WeFollow, and Twellow. Add yourself to as many directories as you can find under the proper categories and you'll begin to see some users following you from these sites.

Justin Bieber Did Not Get Discovered on YouTube

There are many myths about social media. One of the most prevalent is that pop star Justin Bieber, who posted many videos of himself singing on YouTube, was found by record producers online and magically signed to a recording contract. The truth is much more mundane. Yes, Bieber promoted himself on YouTube and also appeared at local talent shows and performed at his school in London, Ontario.

His manager did find him on YouTube.

But he wasn't signed by a major producer or record label that way. On the Howard Stern Show, recording artist and producer Usher dispelled that fantasy. It was actually a personal meeting in a parking lot. Or as the old-timers say, shoe leather and determination. From the Stern Show website:

> "That was an opportunity brought to me," Usher explained, adding that he first encountered Justin in a parking lot. Bieber wanted to audition right then and there, but Usher knew better than to let that happen. The reason: he tried to do the same thing years earlier for record producer Dallas Austin. As a teenager, Usher once stopped Austin in a nightclub parking lot and requested to sing for him, but he declined. Usher wanted to hear Bieber perform but knew it would be best if they did it in a formal setting.
>
> "Let's just do it the right way," Usher told Justin. Later he showed one of Justin's videos to L.A. Reid's ex-wife, Perri "Pebbles" Reid.

Figure 2.7. A popular myth promoted by social media gurus is that Justin Bieber was discovered on YouTube, demonstrating the "value" of social media. He wasn't.

- **Guest blog or blog about your Twitter account:** This strategy works very well if you can give readers an incentive to follow you.

- **Create a video tutorial:** Creating video tutorials for your area of expertise is a great way to get "relevant" exposure for yourself. Place your Twitter username in various places in the video, including the end, and if people feel they have learned something from you then they may be inclined to follow you.

- **Speak at conferences:** The next time you're giving a presentation at a seminar or conference, mention your Twitter account. If you're using presentation software or an on-screen image during your speech, display your username on screen.

The open secret about Twitter and other social media is the existence of armies of fake users, bots, and fans. In 2018 the *New York Times* explored these phenomena in a story titled "The Follower Factory." According to the *Times*, "The accounts are counterfeit coins in the booming economy of online influence, reaching into virtually any industry where a mass audience – or the illusion of it – can be monetized. Fake accounts, deployed by governments, criminals and entrepreneurs, now infest social media networks. By some calculations, as many as 48 million of Twitter's reported active users – nearly 15 percent – are automated accounts designed to simulate real people."

The reasons for buying fake followers are obvious. The Times goes on to say, "High follower counts are also critical for so-called influencers, a budding market of amateur tastemakers and YouTube stars where advertisers now lavish billions of dollars a year on sponsorship deals. The more people influencers reach, the more money they make. . . . an influencer might earn an average of $2000 for a promotional tweet, while an influencer with a million followers might earn $20,000."

How Do I Contact Journalists?

This is a tricky subject. Some PR experts say that it's a great idea to approach journalists on Twitter. Others, including me, are highly skeptical. Some reporters are happy to communicate on Twitter, others are turned off.

First, the Yes answer: "I get 1,000 emails a day," says Grant Marek of *Chubbies*, a former journalist for *Thrillist* and the *San Francisco Examiner*. "Why compete with those 999 other emailers when you could shoot me a tweet and compete with nine other people? A zillion times out of a zillion I'll reply back on Twitter and here's why: being forced to distill a pitch down to 280 characters or less is the ultimate PR exercise. It forces PR pros to cut all of the crap (fake quotes from execs, 'Hi there, how was your weekend?' 33 picture attachments nobody could possibly want) and get to the nut of why I should care."

Here's the No response: Jason Feifer, Editor-in-Chief of *Entrepreneur*, says: "Journalists often joke that, like, 75 percent of our Twitter followers are publicists. The other 25 percent are probably bots. That's fine – I realize it makes good business sense for publicists to follow journalists, so you see what we're talking about and are interested in. And occasionally some of those publicists engage like normal Twitter users, replying to me with a joke or comment. That's cool. I'll often tweet back. I've had some publicist friends request me on Facebook, which I'm less into, unless I've really become friendly with the publicist. I think of Facebook as a place just for my friends. And I always get publicists requesting LinkedIn connections with me, which I don't understand at all. Isn't that for people who have actually worked together? I always reject."

Feifer is not a fan of direct pitching on Twitter. "I absolutely hate when PR people pitch me on Twitter. On principle alone, I will never respond or take a look at what they've sent me. Same goes for Facebook, where I've actually been pitched once or twice. These are social places; they're not appropriate places for pitches. Email is the only appropriate pitching medium."

Rick Newman, a columnist for *Yahoo Finance*, falls somewhere between Feifer and Marek. "I don't mind Twitter pitches, although I can't think of a good one I ever got in that format. It's not the method of pitching that's a problem, it's the quality. The vast majority of pitches suck. (Sorry.) A lot of the time you can tell that some hapless PR soul is pitching the way a client instructed him or her to pitch and probably knows it's going nowhere. The bad pitches are the cookie-cutter variety that seem to take no account of what I cover, what's in the news, or what might even constitute news in the first place. If they're bad pitches in person and bad by email, they'll be bad via Twitter. If I ever saw a good pitch on Twitter I'd probably jump on it the same as if it arrived any other way. Sadly, I don't think that's ever happened."

How to Be Taken Seriously on Social Media

Gallup notes in the conclusion to its report, *The Myth of Social Media*, that the media's potential is still being debated. They report that companies and individuals must follow three main guidelines for a chance at being taken seriously. They must:

- **Be authentic.** Social media sites are highly personal and conversational. And, as Gallup finds, consumers who use these sites do not want to hear sales pitches. They are more likely to listen and respond to companies that seem genuine and personable. They want to interact with a human, not a brand. Companies should back away from the hard sell and focus on creating more of an open dialogue with consumers.

- **Be responsive.** The social media world is 24/7, and consumers expect timely responses – even on nights and weekends. Companies must be available to answer questions and reply to complaints and criticisms. Ignoring negative feedback can do even more damage to a brand's reputation. Instead, companies need to actively listen to what their customers are saying and respond accordingly. If mistakes are made, they must own up to them and take responsibility.

- **Be compelling.** Content is everywhere, and consumers have the ability to pick and choose what they like. Companies have to create compelling, interesting content that appeals to busy, picky social media users. This content should be original to the company and not related to sales or marketing. Consumers need a reason to visit and interact with a company's social media site and keep coming back to it.

Good advice, but hard to implement. As Gallup notes, consumers are finicky, and great content isn't easy to create.

The Dark Side

There's one area of social media, however, that's very effective for public relations – The Dark Side. Shaming and trolling are extremely prevalent.

A lobbyist for the NRA told the *New Yorker* in July 2016 that "Negatives are so much more powerful than positives in politics. I can get people all fired up about something that takes something away. Even if you don't own one of these guns, if they're going to take one away from you, all of a sudden I want to buy one."

Negative emotions are stronger in social media, too.

"Studies have shown that social media is a context where local and small events may escalate into bigger and even global ones in a very short period of time," notes professor Harri Jalonen of Turku University of Applied Sciences, Finland, in his research paper, "Negative Emotions in Social Media as a Managerial Challenge." "A great deal of social media behavior is affected by negativity bias. In psychology, negativity bias refers to a phenomenon in which humans have a greater recall of unpleasant memories compared to positive memories. Adapting it to social media, it means that people are much more likely to recognize and be influenced by negative information shared in social media."

Why does the negative bias dominate? And what does this mean for public relations?

Jon Ronson, in his book *So You've Been Publicly Shamed*, follows victims of social media shaming and humiliation after they've been personally and professionally destroyed on Twitter, Facebook, and other platforms. "We've created this weird surveillance society for ourselves since the advent of social media, where I think we're trying to define each other by the worst tweet we ever wrote," Ronson told National Public Radio. "We're trying to see people's tweets as a kind of clue to their inherent evil, even though we know that's not how human beings actually are."

Dozens of books and articles can be found on the roots of this phenomenon.

Psychology Today magazine identified two main issues: jumping on the self-righteousness bandwagon and bullying. "The *spiral of silence theory* suggests that when people think they are in the majority in a certain setting, they will more freely express their opinion than those who see themselves as in the minority and may fear social ostracism if they express an unpopular opinion," the magazine notes. "Thus, although individuals may not make sexist or racist comments offline, they may feel it's okay to do so in a particular online setting because they think their opinion is the prevalent one there."

The magazine also noted that many commenters on social media are just bullies. "Some individuals are outspoken by nature. Others tend to think that they are morally superior to others. And some just enjoy making other people uncomfortable or angry. Any of these traits may drive individuals to express themselves online without a filter. Personality traits such as self-righteousness and a social dominance orientation (in which you think some social groups, typically yours, are inherently better than others) are related to expressing intolerance. Others are hard-core believers who will express their opinions no matter what, because they believe their opinion is infallible."

If almost any subject can light the dry tinder on a topic that praised and elevated the public relations industry, imagine how many arguments and emotional episodes are begun by topics such as gun control, the Second Amendment, abortion, a new football stadium, an election, religion, or other hot-button issues.

"Shaming, it seems, has become a core competency of the internet, and it's one that can destroy both lives and livelihoods," notes *Wired* magazine. "But the question of who's responsible for the destruction – the person engaging in the behavior or the person revealing it – depends on whom you ask. At its best, social media has given a voice to the disenfranchised, allowing them to bypass the gatekeepers of power and publicize injustices that might otherwise remain invisible. At its worst, it's a weapon of mass reputation destruction, capable of amplifying slander, bullying, and casual idiocy on a scale never before possible."

Author Andreas Ramos has been the victim of several internet trolls, who posted negative comments about him and dared him to respond. "There are thousands of people who try to get visibility and attention by attacking others," said Ramos. "There is nothing that you can say that will stop them; on the contrary, any response will provoke stronger attacks from them. They thrive on controversy. Attacks are a good sign; you're becoming big enough to get attention. Just ignore them."

The dilemma offers no easy answers: respond or ignore.

The U.K. newspaper the *Guardian* offers some great advice on trolling and social media posters who play the blame game in an article titled, "How to Deal with Trolls."

- **Know your troll.** A troll is someone who persistently seeks to derail rational discourse through mindless abuse, needling, hectoring, or even threats of violence. A troll is not someone who disagrees with you, dislikes your work, or disapproves of your moral choices. That's an idiot.

- **The line is not always so easy to draw.** There is a gray area between spirited dissent and out-and-out trolling that houses the passionately misinformed, the casually profane, schoolchildren taking the piss, and otherwise intelligent people who don't put spaces after commas. For the sake of convenience this group is often referred to as "the internet."

- **Don't feed the trolls.** Trolling is one of those rare problems best handled by ignoring it – if you do, it usually goes away. Trolls want your attention and discomfiture; they feed on your impotent rage. If they're trying to be funny, your willingness to rise to the bait provides the punchline. If you don't, there's no joke. The secret to withholding attention is consistency.

To summarize, then, here are the best ways to deal with the dark side of social media:

- **Don't be a troll.** There are only so many hours in the day. You can find more productive pursuits.

Trolling is probably not good for business, and customers and potential clients can see your activities. And as Confucius said, "The angry man is always full of poison." Don't be that person. And remember, trolls, you could be wrong. Then you will attract your own trolls.

- **Don't be a bandwagon-jumper.** Trolls are known to attack to protect their egos and exercise their self-righteousness. You could be next. And trolls are often wrong – you may be on the bad side of an argument. And, again, there are only so many hours in the day.

- **If the attacks are personal, try to ignore them.** As the *Guardian* and *AdWeek* noted, many critics feed on attention, and starving them of this oxygen may encourage them to troll elsewhere.

- **If the attacks are professional, try to reason with the offended commenter via email and take the conversation off social media.** If the troll refuses to be reasonable, you can block or ignore them, ask a third-party advocate to reasonably state your position without engaging the troll, or change the conversation by posting a new blog or column on a completely different issue. This is possible if you're on *Forbes*, *Huffington Post*, etc., or if you have a blog or corporate presence with very compelling content.

Speaking of compelling stories and information leads us to our next chapter, Content Marketing.

CHAPTER 3

Content Marketing

Good writing is supposed to evoke sensation in the reader – Not the fact that it is raining, but the feeling of being rained upon.
— E. L. Doctorow

EVERYBODY LOVES A GOOD STORY. Most people like free advice, especially when it's delivered by an expert.

Or do they? as Keith Morrison on NBC's *Dateline* would say.

The flood of content marketing and digital information often soaks our laptops, phones, screens, TVs, radios, magazines, and newspapers, splashing us in a sea of data that drowns us in friendly, pseudo-sales talk.

Everyone's heard of the phrase. Most people know it's free advice delivered on blogs, news outlets, videos, and similar formats. Indirect. Low pressure. Free information.

"Content marketing is the publication of material designed to promote a brand, usually through a more oblique and subtle approach than that of traditional push advertising," notes the WhatIs website. "The essence is that it offers something the viewer wants, such as information or entertainment. Content marketing can take a lot of different forms, including YouTube videos, blog posts, and articles. It shouldn't really seem like marketing – in some cases, in fact, it should only be identifiable as marketing because the advertiser is identified as the content provider."

Despite the subtle approach and the ultimate goals of sales somewhere down the line, content marketing can be an effective form of public relations, an effort to improve reputation and bolster prominence.

But does it work?

That's the main question public relations professionals, entrepreneurs, and agencies should ask as they consider the time, energy, and cost of building a new website, creating a magazine, or building a series of podcasts or webcasts.

Jacob Silverman, a freelance journalist, author, and a content marketing expert who wrote corporate stories as "paid content," says small guys are disadvantaged.

"I think it's tough for individuals or small businesses to make an impact if they're on one of the big platforms," Silverman says. "Your content may just be lost in a sea of material, especially when larger companies can afford to promote their content and buy ads against searches. There's always a degree of skepticism among readers and customers too, a sense that they're often being sold and pandered to, so I think any content marketing has to feel somehow 'authentic,' which itself is a pretty subjective designation."

Silverman adds, "I struggle to think of any small companies that do this in an effective way, but perhaps they're out there. One key might be to have the article, video, or whatnot able to stand on its own, to have something interesting or meaningful to say, rather than just being a vehicle for brand promotion. If some people realize, 'Oh this hardware store has a useful blog about home improvements,' it could be a nice sell (as well as a way for a store to show its products in action). But a lot of businesses or individuals don't have the time, resources, or creativity to make anything more meaningful than boring listicles or articles laden with advice or tips that can be found anywhere."

The key to standing out is originality. Without it, no one will be influenced, and authors will be ignored.

Two main points everyone needs to consider before tapping a single keystroke:

- You must create *useful content.*
- This useful content must be targeted toward a specific audience.

In a LinkedIn marketing guide, the site offers the usual "rah-rah you-can-do-it" attitude designed to encourage more stories, more seminars, more podcasts created by individuals and businesses. Not coincidentally, these projects may result in more views on their platform.

Think of it as a free salad. The content provider hopes that you like it, which then encourages you to pay for an entrée, two glasses of wine, and dessert. For two. Then tomorrow you'll come back for more, tell your friends, and everyone brings their wallets.

With so many competitors, getting noticed has become incredibly difficult. Content marketing is ubiquitous today because most of it is free, and it's easy to produce. Since it has become so easy, everyone is doing it.

The Beginnings of Content Marketing

Content is common. And content marketing is everywhere. But it's not new.

Before the internet, before TV, and even before radio, content marketing began with tractors, farmers, tires, tobacco, and even a little bit of gelatin.

Baseball Cards

Tobacco companies may have started the trend back in the 1880s, although what they did may not technically meet the definition. According to *Collectors Weekly*, "Cigarette cards were first produced in the 1870s as a means to stiffen flimsy cigarette packs. Initially they were blank until an American businessman thought advertisements should be placed on them. Soon, companies began putting everyone from kings and queens to actresses and baseball players on cards. By the mid-1880s, manufacturers decided to make sets of cards with pithy advertisements on the backs. It was a good way to build customer loyalty since many customers felt compelled to complete their sets!"

The first tobacco company to feature individual athletes may have been Allen & Ginter of Richmond, Virginia. Dave Jamieson, author of *Mint Condition*, notes that the 1888 cigarette packs included the World's Champions series with ten separate cards. They also printed cars of

Figure 3.1. Baseball card featuring Ty Cobb of the Detroit Tigers on the front and marketing for Polar Bear Tobacco on the back, circa 1910. An early example of content marketing.

boxers, wrestlers, billiard players, and gunslingers such as Buffalo Bill and Annie Oakley.

The Baseball Almanac reports that cards became valuable after the turn of the century. "In the T206 set is the famous Honus Wagner card, which is considered the pinnacle of card collecting. According to some historians, Wagner did not want his name on cigarette ads going to kids, so he requested his cards be pulled from the set. Consequently, very few Wagner cards made it into circulation, which makes the T206 Wagner extremely rare. There are other uncommon cards in the set, such as the Eddie Plank, but nothing compares to the scarcity of the Wagner."

In 2013 a Wagner card sold for $2.1 million at auction.

John Deere

If the tobacco cards are considered advertising or general marketing, then the American tractor company John Deere should be considered the first successful content marketer. And possibly the best.

Deere was an inventor and blacksmith famous for creating the first mass-produced steel plow in 1837. It was hardier and more effective than the iron-and-wood plows commonly used. In 1886 Deere passed away but his company continued to grow.

In 1895, a seminal year for content marketing and John Deere, the company's marketing team noticed something very important.

"The same kind of customer who would be likely to purchase a combine harvester would probably be interested in new advances in corn planting," the content marketing firm IMN reported on its website. "So John Deere positioned itself as not only a source of agriculture products, but as a source of agricultural news and information. The company created *The Furrow* magazine, an agricultural publication full of news, guides, and information for farmers. Calling *The Furrow* a success would be an understatement; it's still in circulation to this day, with a subscriber base of over one million farmers in 40 countries."

Deere sowed the seeds of loyalty by educating its base.

"What made *The Furrow* so successful was exactly what makes non-marketing publications successful: the strength

Figure 3.2. Cover of an 1897 issue of the magazine *The Furrow,* produced by John Deere. An early example of content marketing, the magazine positioned the company as a source of valuable information that created considerable customer loyalty.

of the content," IMN says. "*The Furrow* became extremely popular in the agricultural community because it offered useful insight, important information, and essential trade news. This wasn't a glorified advertisement; it was valuable agricultural journalism provided by one of the industry's top companies. By positioning itself as the publisher, John Deere was able to foster customer loyalty, spread the brand's message, and gain even more respect and traction in a competitive industry."

Here's a front-page story on *The Furrow* website about a cattle ranch in Hawaii:

> One April morning on the Hawaiian island of Maui, the manager of Haleakala Ranch, Greg Friel, and his son and grandson saddle up to herd cattle from one lush pasture to another. Eight thousand feet above them looms the mountain's crater, invisible among frothing clouds; two thousand feet below, the Pacific Ocean sparkles under sunny skies to the horizon. Meanwhile, 16 miles away, the manager of Ulupalakua Ranch, Jimmy Gomes, is driving southward on the mid-mountain Pi'ilani Highway. He emerges from a bucolic forest onto terrain that looks like rural southern Italy, then enters territory that's drier still — a bed of hard basalt lava that spilled thousands of years ago from cracks in the earth. Gomes follows the road through more greenery where it dips to the ocean's edge. He parks at Kaupo Ranch, where manager Bobby

Ferreira has gathered some prized Angus derivative bulls to sell. The two make a deal.

What deal? What cattle? Why Hawaii? I want to read more. That's good old-fashioned premium prose, something we should all aspire to produce.

Michelin

Five years after *The Furrow* grooved into the American Midwest, a French tire company rolled into history and revolutionized content marketing in Europe.

According to a handy history provided by the Michelin Group, within hours after a request was made (helpful public relations? check), the first *Michelin Guide* appeared in 1900. At the time there were fewer than 3000 cars in France.

"To encourage the development of the industry, and consequently, the demand for tires and other Michelin products, the brothers decided to offer motorists a document which would facilitate their travels, a small guide to improve mobility," according to Michelin. "The first edition of the *Michelin Guide* saw the light of day in August 1900 with nearly 35,000 copies printed. . . . This *Guide*, handed out at no charge to motorists, held an array of practical information and tips, such as how to use and repair tires, where to find hotels and petrol stations, maps, and a list of mechanics, since there were fewer than 600 of them in all of France at the time. In 1904, a first guide was published outside of France: the *Michelin Guide Belgium*."

The guides focused on basic repair tips and maps to hotels and gas stations and was basically unchanged until 1920. That year the founder, André Michelin, visited a tire store and found his guides propping up a workbench. That was the end of the free guides. Michelin noted,

"Man only truly respects what he pays for!" Advertisements were removed and a list of hotels in Paris also debuted.

Other notable milestones for Michelin:

1926 – The first fine dining star begins.

1929 – A satisfaction questionnaire is included with the guide asking readers to comment.

1931 – The second and third stars debuted criteria (one star: a very good restaurant in its own category; two stars: excellent cooking, worth a detour; and three stars: exceptional cuisine, worth a special trip).

2005 – The *Michelin Guide* comes to America – *New York Michelin*, with 500 restaurants listed.

2006 – The second guide debuts in the United States in San Francisco.

Jell-O

Early content marketing wasn't all tires and tractors. In 1904, Jell-O was promoted through demonstrations of the product in stores, and free recipe books were distributed by the thousands, which resulted in a massive jump in sales. Free recipe books are common today, but the unique concept wowed consumers in the days before jazz, TV, and the interstate highway system.

The Furrow and the Michelin Guides continue today, in print and online. They enjoy first-mover advantages and

Figure 3.3. Cover of the first regional *Michelin Guide,* from 1926, which covered Brittany. Image courtesy of Michelin.

huge name recognition, plus credibility. They enjoy a century-plus head start. They are supported by brands, publicists, distribution systems, and other advantages that no small business could possibly compete with or overcome. But competition may be even harder today. Why?

Content Marketing Challenges

Since the barriers on the internet are almost zero, anyone can, and most companies do, produce content.

Many large organizations, such as Cision, Meltwater, PR Newswire, and the Content Marketing Institute, actively promote content marketing. And why not? It's their business and they believe in it. Ask the California Avocado Commission for a recommendation of what fruit to add to your diet. Or ask the International Coffee Organization if they want consumers to drink more tea.

The unabashed promotion of content marketing doesn't mean it works for everyone or, in fact, for anyone. Take their advocacy with several grains of salt, sugar, and some avocados, too.

The Content Marketing Institute is a group that provides white papers, major conferences, webinars, e-books, and other resources. "Our mission is to advance the practice of content marketing. While the site is full of practical, how-to guidance, you'll also find insight and advice from the experts, and an active community for discussing the latest news, information, and advances that are moving the industry forward."

Joe Pulizzi, the founder of the Content Marketing Institute, promotes a utopian vision in the LinkedIn marketing guide. "It's democratic. Anyone, anywhere, with any budget, can develop a valuable audience over time and make an impact. In other words, there are no excuses for not doing this well, as long as you have a plan and execute against that plan."

With all due respect, this is highly optimistic. Here are several reasons why.

- If anyone could do it, everything would go viral. Everyone would be famous. A study by Sharad Goel and Ashton Anderson of Stanford University and Jake Hofman and Duncan Watts, in the January 2016 edition of *Management Science*, debunks the myth of easy viral growth or peer-to-peer sharing. "We find that structural virality is typically low, and remains so independent of size, suggesting that popularity is largely driven by the size of the largest broadcast." In a summary of the preliminary research of the study in the *MIT Sloan Management Review*, the writer noted that viral growth is a fantasy since 99 percent of the time multistep diffusion dies out after one generation.

- Content marketing is a zero-sum game. There are only so many people on their computers, tablets, or phones at the same time. If your business grabs attention, it's probably not from new users leaving their TV sets, books, movies, or sports activities. They are coming from another website or source.

- It's not democratic. Try to compete against Michelin, John Deere, Jell-O, American Express, or any other behemoth. Do you have the same resources? The same brand recognition?

- What plan? To get five new customers? 5,000? An interview on the *Today Show*? The statement is too generic to be useful.

In an article titled "Content Marketing Doesn't Work Like You Think It Does," in *Cirrus Insight* magazine, Joshua Loomis tosses a bucket of water on the feel-good bonfire.

> A lot of content marketing 'gurus' make the job sound like all you need to do is spit out 50 high-quality blog posts and share them on social and then you'll have a top blog for the business sector. You put out the content, get a few shares, people will check it out, want the extra content you have, and before you know it you'll be drowning in leads.
>
> Not quite. Blog awareness can vary widely by who your audience is and where you're able to get featured. A great blog can go for years without breaking into the big time. When it finally does start helping the business, it'll be because of people who have read your content multiple times and are starting to have a relationship with your company.
>
> Someone can find one of your articles and have months go by before they finally give you any contact information or make a purchase from you. Until you slowly build up to having a huge audience your content won't be converting much, but the goal shouldn't be strictly converting. The goal needs to be gaining brand awareness

and increasing customer interaction in any fashion. Something a lot of companies struggle with is not creating the content, but spreading it.

Here are some more buzz killers. David Spark of Spark Media Solutions debunked the utopian vision via his article in *Social Media Biz*. "It's insidious," he says. "It says here's some content for you that you'll find valuable. But when you're not looking, we're going to sell you something. There's no marketing. When you create content to inform and educate, you're providing an answer that may fulfill a step in the sales process, and you may be strengthening trust of your brand, but that's true of all content. You read a book by a certain author and if you like it, you'll be compelled to purchase and read their next book. Each article in a newspaper must be of a certain quality. If it's not, you will stop reading and purchasing the newspaper."

Those who expect magical unicorn results by posting a single video, presentation, graphic or article will always be disappointed. "Companies feel they only need to do one video or one article and test it," says Spark. He says many firms hear about someone else's video going viral with three million hits and believe they too can hit a grand slam home run in their first time at bat.

Spark compares quality content marketing to a very good television show, newspaper, or magazine. "Did any of these successful magazines or TV shows post *one* article or *one* TV show?" Spark tells clients they must commit to a series of programming. One-shots simply don't work.

Author and online marketer Neil Patel (*Crazy Egg* and *Hello Bar*) preaches the disciplines of consistency and quality production, aka volume. "The quickest way to kill a content marketing campaign is to have zero content," Patel notes. "Or to start to produce content and then stop. I've seen this happen way too many times." He says, "Failure strikes some time after the launch of content marketing. The excitement that initially fueled content marketing gives way to the weariness of producing it. It could be a couple weeks. It could be a few months. Content marketing demands consistency. You can't just throw a bunch of content on the web and expect it to generate traffic for the long haul. Search engines prefer to rank sites that show signs of life. You'll reap maximum SEO benefit if you produce fresh content consistently."

Bad vs. Good Content Marketing

Bad content marketing may do more harm than good.

Deanne Taenzer of ExpertFile, a marketing platform to promote experts online, warns entrepreneurs not to publish anything, anywhere, at any time. "I'm a purist and not of the regime that everyone can write and all content is good," Taenzer says. "I like relevant content from people who can articulate the value succinctly and with great grammar and punctuation. When I see poor writing, I turn off and stop reading. And let's be real, there is a lot of poor writing and useless dribble on LinkedIn, Facebook, and Medium."

Taenzer says she's not a total Debbie Downer on self-produced content. "What I do believe is if a small business or an entrepreneur is solving a problem, there is worth to their voices and their content. As long as their voice is used to contribute value, or more directly, to solve that problem."

Differences in Content Marketing

Good Content Marketing	Bad Content Marketing
Helpful	Self-serving
Informational	Promotional
Original	Derivative
Realistic	Unicorn fantasy
Subtle	Obvious
Like reading a good magazine	Like seeing an advertisement
Specific	Overly general

Figure 3.4. You need to be aware of the differences between good and bad content marketing. Bad content marketing can actually do harm.

Good content serves some of the same functions as public relations – building reputation, enhancing trust, and establishing the author as an expert. Here's what PR Newswire has to say:

> The practice of public relations is about influencing public opinion and guarding reputation. Content marketing is focused ultimately on outcomes like lead generation and sales. In terms of the old marketing funnel describing the different stages in the buying cycle (awareness, consideration, preference, choice) construct, PR is arguably more 'upper funnel,' because it builds

awareness and reputation. Content marketing is positioned deeper within the cycle, in the realms of consideration and choice. . . . This is why content marketing and public relations are suddenly finding themselves elbow-to-elbow in the communications mix and the strategy. Both rely heavily on publishing messages with the goal of influencing opinion and generating specific outcomes. Both disciplines also benefit mightily from the connectedness of our audiences via social media, as well as the new weight that search engines are placing on fresh content. Good messaging can gain traction quickly and spread virally across networks of people connected by common interests.

Good analysis, but with one caveat. No matter how much content marketing you create, it's rarely as powerful as public relations. Remember the section on PR vs. advertising. PR = reporters and trusted media outlets reporting stories about you and your client. Self-produced content = look how great we are!

Author Andreas Ramos, author of *The Big Book of Content Marketing*, notes "The little guys have a huge disadvantage because they're the little guys. Big brands, strong logos, etc. will dominate in the mass market. Most social media experts, bloggers, authors, etc., plus the heads of large social companies, overinflated the value of social. The same happened in content marketing. A few companies promised Shangri-la. But the reality of content: it is hard work, very difficult to build and collect metrics, etc. And it's very, very (too) easy to puff it as 'brand marketing,' which means lots of billing, lots of noise, and no metrics."

Content Marketing Formats

There are billions of social media posts every day. How do individuals and small businesses make an impact? Today writers can produce content in the following formats:

- **Blog posts.** These can be personal websites, social media accounts, LinkedIn, *Medium*, and other non-edited, anyone-can-write (and they do!) venue. These are the most common and least effective forms of communication. As we saw in the previous section on social media, there are almost five billion items of "content" posted daily on Facebook, five billion videos are watched every day on YouTube, and 500 million Tweets are sent each day, along with 130,000 posts per week on LinkedIn. As Groucho Marx said, "I wouldn't want to be part of any club that would have me as a member." Maybe Groucho was speaking about those long articles on *Medium*, or personal posts or articles on LinkedIn. Nobody cares beyond your office mates, parents, and very close friends, and they're probably clicking like or recommend just to make you feel good.

- **Edited blog posts.** *Forbes*, *Huffington Post*, and others. Here's a quick rule – the harder it is to obtain, the more prestigious and impactful it is. Do you have an editorial or monthly slot in the *New York*

Times or *Wall Street Journal*? You don't need to read this chapter. For writers, being on the *Huffington Post* or *Forbes* helps with credibility and reach, up to a point. For example, my most popular column on *Forbes* has more than 450,000 views. On Facebook or LinkedIn, I'm lucky to get 5 or 10 views. Not 5 or 10 thousand, 5 or 10 *total*. But there are more than 1,000 contributors and staffers now on *Forbes*, and hundreds more, maybe thousands, on *Entrepreneur, Inc., Huffington Post*, and others. The party is a lot less exclusive than when I started my column in 2009. Writers hoping to build an audience face stiff competition with more-established contributors and from the paid writers who get premium placement on those websites.

- **Editorials.** These are opinionated stories, often written in the first person, designed to take a specific position rather than an objective presentation ("both sides") on a current news story.

- **Video (mostly YouTube).** Everybody likes fun short videos of wacky cats, wacky stunts, cute cats, cute kids, offensive comedy, and sex (PG, R, and X). But for building brands and promoting products, finding an audience can be a challenge. Without a professional and sometimes expensive production, breaking through the clutter is very rare. Here are five solid tips on creating and promoting videos:

  1. **Pay attention to tone.** "It should reflect your tone of voice," says Michelle Messenger Garrett of Garrett Public Relations. "And you

should know the goal behind the video. What are you trying to achieve?"

2. **Have some humor.** "A good video in content marketing without the need to spend a lot of money should revolve around an idea that makes people say something to the effect of, 'I should have thought of that,'" says Neal Rodriguez, a *Forbes* contributor and online marketing expert. In 2015 Rodgriguez pranked his two children by promising them Transformers toys and filmed them opening the Amazon boxes to find vegetables. Their howls of outrage were shown on national TV, and Rodriguez' phone blew up with new potential clients.

3. **Show emotion.** "So often corporate videos are devoid of emotion because they're so heavily scripted, prepared, or just spouting out marketing jargon," says David Spark. "My favorite part of video, and what can make a great video, is when you watch people *react*. Take a look at the reality shows and look at how many times they cut away to reaction shots, and how the reaction alone can tell far more about what the person said than the actual words that came out of their mouth. For that reason, I like to produce funny 'man on the street' videos where I purposely go out of my way to ask the question you're not supposed to ask. For example, at the RSA security show I've asked people to give me their password. At VMworld, I've

asked people how they explain virtualization to their mom. And at Dreamforce, I've asked people "When is the best time to swear at your customers?" Watch the videos and you'll see there are lots of people simply reacting to the question. You want to spark a conversation in the industry, these kinds of videos do it."

4. **Share your video.** "Creating compelling content that will resonate with your target audience is critical, but it's equally important to have a plan in place for amplifying that content across channels," says Kevin Akeroyd, CEO of Cision. "Today's consumers are increasingly swayed by influencers and social connections; ensure that you're connecting with these individuals to get your content shared and promoted. Avoid having content 'stand alone' and create a multichannel approach that covers earned, owned, and paid media. Before it's even published, you should develop a promotion strategy, again leveraging insights to uncover who the influencers are who will help it get noticed. Then use data to find the top performing content and continue sharing with updated messaging to hit more key audiences."

- **Podcasts.** These are audio recordings of interviews, feature stories, and other subjects similar to a radio feature. They can be popular with celebrity hosts, but it's a challenge to attract ears and minds in a short-attention-span world.

- **Webinars and teleseminars.** Live presentations, they often work best when the guest is invited by a company with a large, built-in audience.

- **Slide presentations or tutorials.** The internet is flooded with charts, graphs, and other visual information packets.

- **Free e-books.** These can be a tremendous amount of work for very little return. Self-published books are the lonely orphans of the digital world. Better to try shorter content first before attempting a major endeavor.

- **Newsletters.** With the proper email lists and timely distribution, this is one of the few avenues with promise. Here are some solid tips from the Vertical Response Blog and Hubspot regarding the science of building newsletters.

    1. **No surprises.** "Let them know what value they can expect from you in your newsletters," notes Vertical Response. "That may be bi-weekly discounts on certain items, or invites to high-tech events. Whatever it is, let them know the frequency and the general content they can expect to receive upfront. When there are no surprises, your readers may be less likely to unsubscribe from your emails."

    2. **Be gentle.** "Your email inbox is like your front door," notes Vertical Response. "The more someone knocks, the more you want to pretend you're not home! Let's be honest, no one wants to be the annoying (albeit well-meaning)

neighbor who drops by a little too often. Stick with the mailing frequency you promised at the time someone subscribed, and if you plan to change it and mail more often, let them know so they can decide if they want to stay on your list. By providing valuable content and mailing when you're expected to, you'll be welcome in your subscribers' inboxes."

3. **Be balanced.** Hubspot notes, "Your newsletter content should be 90 percent educational and 10 percent promotional. Chances are, your email newsletter subscribers don't want to hear about your products and services 100 percent of the time. While they may love you and want to hear from you, there's only so much shilling you can do before they tune out."

4. **Start strong.** "You have about 50 (give or take) characters to nail your subject line," notes Vertical Response. "Your subject line should be a clear, concise reflection of what's in your email. It should be attention-getting to stand out. . . . Don't waste any time getting to the good stuff!"

5. **Be transparent.** "Get specific," HubSpot says. "Tell potential subscribers exactly what will be in the newsletter as well as how often they should expect to hear from you."

Paul Gillin, in a widely cited presentation, "Create Stuff They've Just Gotta Read: How to Write for Social Networks," offers 15 ways to organize a blog post or article. He uses the subject of privacy as an example.

1. Quiz. Test Your Privacy IQ.

2. Skeptic. You Don't Control Your Privacy Any More.

3. Explainer. The Online Privacy Debate in Plain English.

4. Case Study. How One Person Got Control Over Privacy.

5. Contrarian. Why Online Privacy Concerns Are Overblown.

6. How-To. Five Steps to Improving Online Privacy.

6.5 Quick-How-To. Three Stupid Simple Things You Can Do to Keep Your Profile Private.

7. How NOT To. Five Ways to Compromise Your Online Privacy.

8. First Person. My Personal Privacy Horror Story.

9. Comparison. How Privacy Protection Services Measure Up.

10. Q&A. Five Common Questions About Online Privacy with Edward Snowden.

11. Data. Are Privacy Problems Worsening? Yes, Says Survey.

12. Man on the Street. Experts Offer Opinions on the State of Online Privacy.

13. Outrageous. Why Online Privacy Is an Oxymoron.

13.5 *BuzzFeed*-Style Outrageous (not advised but good for a laugh!). This Woman Insists Online Privacy is a Joke, and You Won't Believe What Happened Next.

14. Insider Secrets. The One Thing You Need to Know About Your Online Privacy.

15. Literary Treatment. Online privacy haiku, epic narrative poem, comic book treatment, or whatever else your imagination can muster.

Even with all this great advice, author Andreas Ramos says, "Only the top 1–2 percent of content will be visible. The remaining 98 percent of content in that niche will sink beneath the waves, never to be seen. Quite simply because nobody wants #4 or #56. Everyone wants #1. Look at the Olympics: #1 is the winner, #2 is the near-winner, and #3 is whatever. Who cares about #4? Who cares about the rest of the field, and the hundreds, if not thousands, who didn't qualify for the Olympics?"

Like social media, which is often a mirage, most content marketing doesn't work. Too common. Too poorly written. Wrong distribution channels. Nobody cares.

Tony Halle, CEO of Chartbeat, a data analytics company that consults for *Time* magazine and many other publishers, says get to the point. "If you're an average reader, I've got your attention for 15 seconds," Halle notes. "We're getting a lot wrong about the web these days. We confuse what people have clicked on for what they've read. We mistake sharing for reading. We race toward new trends like advertising without fixing what was wrong with the old ones and make the same mistakes all over again."

Halle believes there are at least three major myths about content marketing. What the gurus and hipsters are selling the masses isn't necessarily true.

His research found that:

- People don't always read what they click. "Most people who click don't read. In fact, a stunning 55 percent spent fewer than 15 seconds actively on a page."

- Social sharing is pretty meaningless. "The people who share content are a small fraction of the people who visit that content. Among articles we tracked with social activity, there were only one tweet and eight Facebook likes for every 100 visitors."

- Paid content, or "native advertising," is probably a waste of money. "The truth is that while the emperor that is native advertising might not be naked, he's almost certainly only wearing a thong. On a typical article two-thirds of people exhibit more than 15 seconds of engagement, on native ad content that plummets to around one-third. . . . On the native content we analyzed, only 24 percent of visitors scrolled down the page at all, compared with 71 percent for normal content."

The research above contradicts the theory that one secret to successful content marketing is to pay for it. With the journalism industry in a long, slow death spiral, many companies such as *Conde Nast* and the *New York Times*, along with *Buzzfeed*, *Mashable*, and other online publications, offer "sponsored content" that looks like news stories.

This is not something most people read about in feel-good articles or "everyone can be successful" blogging conferences.

Freelance journalist Jacob Silverman delved into this practice in his article in *The Baffler* magazine. "Legacy publishers are following *BuzzFeed*'s lead, heeding the call of the digital co-marketers and starting in-house, sponsored-content shops of their own. *CNN* opened one last spring, and its keepers, with nary a trace of self-awareness, dubbed it 'Courageous.' The *New York Times* has T Brand Studio (clients include Dell, Shell, and Goldman Sachs), the S.I. Newhouse empire has something called 23 stories by *Conde Nast*, and the *Atlantic* has Re:think. . . . The promise is that quality promotional content will sit cheek-by-jowl with traditional journalism, aping its style and leveraging its prestige without undermining its credibility."

In addition to the promise of exposure, these stories promise something most articles cannot hope to provide – quality writing by journalists on staff or talented freelancers.

But this isn't cheap. Here are some prices found for such advertorial copy that allows brands to claim, "As seen in *GQ*" or "Appearing in the *Washington Post*" or "Paid For and Posted by" in the *New York Times*.

- *Forbes*: "Special Features campaign is $100,000 per month, with a two-month minimum. The unlimited publishing feature BrandVoice Elite costs $75,000 per month, with a four-month minimum; and BrandVoice Stories, which includes four paid stories over a two-month period, goes for $50,000." (*Advertising Age*)

- *New York Times*' T-Brand Studio: Prices are estimated to begin at $100,000 and can quickly go higher. (*Advertising Age*)

- BI Intelligence Interactive Advertising Bureau says native ads will make $21 billion in ad spending in 2018 – four times more than 2013.

- Average price? $54,000 (*Daily Egg*)

One of the most expensive, and possibly the best-written and most lushly produced content, comes from the *New York Times*' T-Brand Studio. (T-Brand Studio was launched in 2014, and it has quickly grown to more than 200 people.) Take the campaign for the investment bank and financial services firm UBS, "AI: What It Takes to Be Human," a multimedia exploration of artificial intelligence from the perspective of Nobel Prize winners.

Starting with text gently layered over soft, futuristic images, the story begins:

> This year marks the 100th anniversary of the birth of Herbert A. Simon, a Nobel laureate in economics "for his groundbreaking research into the decision-making process within economic organizations." Simon was also a visionary in the area of artificial intelligence, and his first notable work in the field, "The Logic Theory Machine," from 1956, is celebrating its 60th anniversary in 2016. Co-created with Allen Newell, it described the first computer program designed to simulate the problem-solving skills of humans.

Building on Simon's achievements in the field of artificial intelligence, we take a journey to explore the latest innovations in AI and, most importantly, its human element, to ultimately answer the controversial questions: What physical human characteristics and emotions must a robot have to make people react to it? And, obversely, can AI recognize human emotions?

As the story builds via text and images, readers are invited to scroll down to where a short film appears, immersing the audience deeper and deeper into the subject.

In the three-minute film, shot in Japan in the style of *Blade Runner 2049*, Professor Hiroshi Ishiguro from Osaka University delves into questions of consciousness and thought as he builds a near-human robot, Erica, in his lab. Then the journey continues with more text, more chapters in the story, more images, and more film. It's a multimedia learning experience that redefines traditional advertising and marketing.

But this type of production not for everyone. It's simply too expensive for many smaller firms.

Adam Aston, Vice President and Executive Editorial Director for T-Brand Studio, explains that costs can rise to seven figures for production alone. "As we've been asked to go further and further and higher and higher and places we've never gone before, that means big money." Besides the $1M+ production price tag, the advertiser must also pay for the placement in the *New York Times*, which can run an additional $2 for every $1 in production.

Figure 3.5. Opening page of "AI: What It Takes to Be Human," from the *New York Times*, branded content paid for and posted by USB and designed by T-Brand Studio. Courtesy of USB.

The philosophy of "AI: What It Takes to Be Human," as one example of "richly-designed story pages," can be explained by Aston as a new way of telling stories that look different from regular news articles, photos, and videos. "We make sure that branded content and newsroom content are different," Aston says. The differentiation includes different fonts and labeling the content as paid or branded. "The brand partners want great richness and greater functionality than a newsroom story. We are routinely building pages with animated illustrations, dynamic charts, videos, immersive images, animated gifs, and the richest aspects of web design at the moment."

For the near future, Aston predicts even bigger productions featuring virtual reality, augmented reality, and other technologies.

The actual stories created are beyond the usual "Buy My Product!" Using UBS as an example, the "AI: What It Takes . . ." marketing never mentions retirement planning or stock trading. "Financial companies have a challenge to distinguish themselves with similar products and services," Aston says. "How do you talk to consumers about why you are different? That kind of affiliation showing expertise with exotic technology and future ideas sheds a beneficial light by promoting progressive ideas."

The Washington Post offers similar services to the *New York Times* with their native advertising department, Brand Studio. Brand Studio boldly challenges their advertisers, most of them very large and powerful companies: "Influencing the influencers requires rich, immersive content with value and a point of view. The story always comes first; it's what

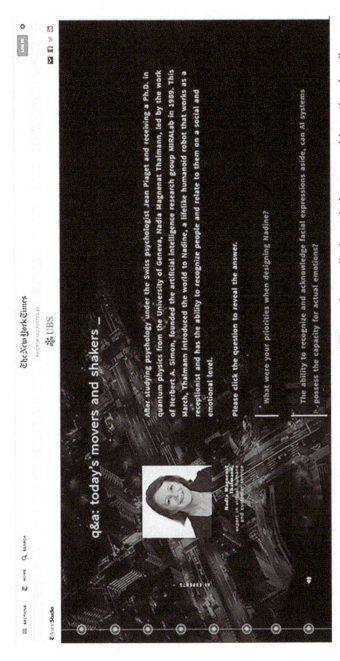

Figure 3.6. Inside page of "AI: What It Takes to Be Human." The reader scrolls through the story – this section describes creating robots capable of recognizing the subtleties of human expressions and emotions. Courtesy of USB.

our audience expects. We focus on the story you want to tell, then couple our investigative chops and immersive storytelling with next-gen tech to tell it – in the very best way for that story."

The product offerings include rich graphics and award-winning writers creating stories layered with video, illustrations, photos, multimedia content, and original podcasts. Perhaps the best example is "The Economics of Change," produced for Dell Technologies and Intel about the future of finance. It's a techno-funhouse filled with short movies, podcasts, illustrations and packets of data on cryptocurrency and the future of money.

Small Businesses and Content Marketing

Author Andreas Ramos offers the best advice for small businesses: *Don't compete with the big boys,* you will lose. Instead, find your own smaller space and make it your own. "There's opportunity in niche markets: a little guy can become an expert and, with a few books, become a superstar within a niche. It's very hard for large brands to control niche markets because they can't specialize/personalize enough. And niche markets aren't trivial; any niche market is worth tens of millions of dollars, which is good for a little guy but trivial for a large company. So, yes, it's possible . . . if you work very hard at it."

David Spark agrees and he advises clients: "Try not to bite off everything, you can't do it if you don't have the bandwidth. Just pick one specific solution."

Here's a great example of a very specific solution. It's a helpful, well-written article from Square. It's fun. It's quick. It challenges conventional wisdom. It's visual. It's simple.

7 Interesting Findings About How (and Why) People Tip

The only magic formula for increasing tips at your business is to provide friendly, exceptional service. But there are a few interesting data points that shed some additional light on why people tip more – and where. Here are seven surprising statistics about customer tipping behavior in the United States:

No. 1: Perhaps because it's such a fast and easy checkout experience, people tip more when they pay with mobile wallets (like Apple Pay and Android Pay).

No. 2: Interestingly, according to a survey by Software Advice, people are more likely to tip if they're required to press a "no tip" button to opt out of tipping.

No. 3: People prefer to use iPads to input tips themselves. Eighty-six percent of respondents in the Software Advice survey indicated this preference.

No. 4: Your location matters. New Hampshire has the most generous tippers in the country – people there tip an average of 17.1 percent on Square Register. And South Dakota is the stingiest – the average tip amount on Square Register there is 15.3 percent.

No. 5: Delaware bar patrons are the most generous in the country – their average tip amount on a tab is 23.6 percent, according to Square data. Virginia comes in last at an average tip amount of 16 percent per bar tab on Square Register.

No. 6: Having your register positioned close to both your cashier/server and customer helps increase tips. Forty-one percent of those surveyed by Software Advice said close proximity to the server or cashier while entering a tip amount would "probably" or "definitely" increase their likelihood to tip.

No. 7: It's the norm to tip pretty high for coffee. Most people in the country tip 19 to 20 percent at coffee shops that use Square.

Here are three more great examples of online content marketing, two from the travel industry, Travel Portland and Vienna: Now and Forever, and one from a new health technology firm, Blu Room Enterprises.

First is a brief example from Travel Portland's wonderfully-designed website, an article titled "7 Only-in-Portland Fall Drinks. Notice the writing. Short. Punchy. Powerful. Flavorful. Makes you thirsty, doesn't it?

AVERAGE TIP ACROSS THE U.S.

Where are tippers most generous? Average customer
tip by state at sellers using Square's tipping screen.

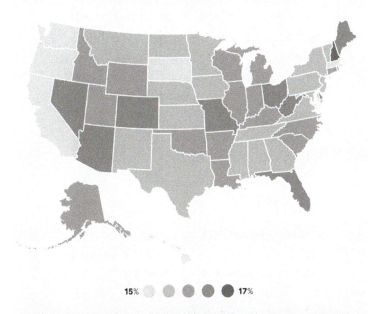

15% ● ● ● ● ● 17%

FIVE LEAST GENEROUS STATES		FIVE MOST GENEROUS STATES	
South Dakota	15.3%	New Hampshire	17.1%
Hawaii	15.4%	Delaware	16.6%
Massachusetts	15.5%	Arizona	16.6%
California	15.6%	Nevada	16.5%
Oregon	15.6%	West Virginia	16.5%

Data from Square, January 2016

Figure 3.7. A powerful visual, like this one from Square (part of the
article on the previous pages), shows how content marketing can help
a company build customer loyalty by providing beneficial information.
Image courtesy of Square.

7 Only-in-Portland Fall Drinks

From pumpkin spice to habanero caramel, Portland's flavorful autumn beverages will leave you thirsty for more.

Before pumpkin spice lattes became seasonal meme fodder, Portland was brewing up creative beverages fitting for fall's crisp weather. Intense spices mixed with rich cream and bitter chocolate; smoky scotch with splashes of cinnamon syrup, ginger, vanilla, clove, and nutmeg; all artfully combine to bring a smile to your lips and warmth in your belly.

Not Boozy

Chai at Tea Chai Te

When searching for perfect fall flavor, it's hard to go wrong with chai. What *is* hard is deciding which one to order at Tea Chai Te. Their pumpkin spice chai mixes cinnamon, ginger, vanilla, clove, and nutmeg (it's basically pumpkin pie in a mug), while their festive gingerbread chai blends notes of brown sugar and ginger, reminiscent of freshly baked holiday cookies. The caramel creme brûlée chai is a full sensory experience, so delicious and decadently aromatic you'll wish it also came as a scented candle. Decisions, decisions . . .

Coconut Cardamom Latte at Dragonfly Coffee House

Step outside the pumpkin spice box and discover why the coconut cardamom latte from Dragonfly Coffee House is the new standard for caffeinated baking-spice beverages. Spicy cardamom playfully resonates throughout, complementing the espresso with a tongue-tickling kick. The coconut syrup's sweet earthiness rounds out the flavor for creamy warmth you'll savor on Portland's cool autumn mornings.

Habanero-Caramel Drinking Chocolate at Xico

Like a black cauldron of witch's brew, the habanero-caramel drinking chocolate at Xico is pure magic. Melted, sinfully dark chocolate gives way to hints of vanilla and fragrant caramel, followed by a warming smack of habanero spice. You'll try to hide the giddy grin, but even the innocent dollop of vanilla cream on top can't conceal the love spell that's just been cast.

Pumpkin Pie Milkshake at Cool Moon Ice Cream

As autumn churns out its final warm days, enjoying a pumpkin pie milkshake from Cool Moon Ice Cream on the nearby fountain steps at Jamison Square becomes a cherished fall memory. Spice it up by adding a scoop of salted caramel or butter pecan ice cream. This chilly, sippable treat is the perfect companion for a shady stroll beneath the neighborhood's falling copper and ruby leaves.

The goal is to promote travel to Portland. The vehicle is the quick beverage roundup. Mission Accomplished.

Now look at another boffo travel site, Vienna Now and Forever. They assault your senses, in a good way, with fast-paced, professionally edited, and quick videos ranging from two to eight minutes for the short attention spans of the modern traveler. The beautiful images serve another purpose – they transcend language. In fact, many of the videos offer translations in several languages. This is not always possible for small businesses, but it's vital for bigger firms with international clients.

Titles of the videos include:

- "Experience Vienna as a Brand" with images of rivers, trees, lush gardens, coffee shops, beautiful people, and world-famous architecture

- "Coffins, Graveyards, and Broken Skulls" features macabre museums with unusual weapons, famous graveyards, and bizarre skeletons

- "Christmas in Vienna" with explosions of colorful holiday lights, holiday music, and thousands of guests enjoying freshly roasted chestnuts and freshly baked cookies.

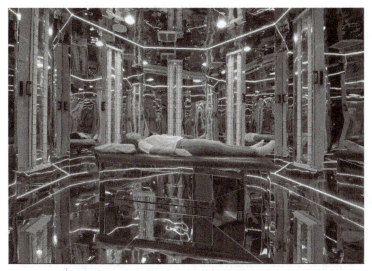

Figure 3.8. Winning photo entry in *National Geographic* of a patient relaxing inside the Blu Room. Courtesy of Rory Sagner Photography ©2018. rory-sagner.pixels.com.

For our final example, the Blu Room is a new treatment to assist with healing and promote relaxation. There are 26 facilities around the world using this patented technology that shields users from the outside world. The sessions consist of 20 minutes of deep relaxation inside a futuristic octagon bathed in blue UVB light (Figure 3.8).

The company, based outside of Seattle, Washington, engages in content marketing by sending emails that summarize appropriate mainstream media stories. Their email list consists of patients, licensees, and sales prospects, and emails are sent once a week or less to prevent inbox fatigue. For example, one email featured a link to a winning photo entry in *National Geographic* of a patient relaxing inside the Blu Room, taken by photographer Rory Sagnar. The credibility of *National Geographic*, along with the beauty of the photo, created a powerful marketing opportunity.

With the plethora of agencies, books, and free advice, anyone can produce decent content marketing.

Stephane Fitch, managing editor of FitchInk and a former bureau chief in Chicago and London for *Forbes*, takes a more pragmatic view of the decline of the traditional media model and believes there's a sunny side to the rise of amateur content.

"What is happening to serious journalism now resembles what happened to poetry a century or two ago," Fitch says. "Remember, the market for verse was quite lucrative for hundreds of years. Homer, Virgil, Pope, Shakespeare, Yeats, and many other, lesser-known bards practiced their craft full-time and earned a solid living. But by the early 1900s, the market was flooded and the audience had largely moved on to novels. Great poets like William Carlos Williams and Wallace Stevens had full-time careers in medicine and insurance, respectively. Robert Frost was an English teacher, as are many fine poets today." He goes on to say that, "What's important is that even though the business model for poetry collapsed, the art of poetry never did. There's magnificent verse being written today for serious readers – by poets who are so committed that they do it almost for free and on their own time. And that's a hopeful thing. I tell people who like to read and write serious journalism this almost daily." Fitch concludes, "The best reporting will be increasingly done out of pure passion, mostly by brilliant people who've worked out other means by which to pay the rent."

Thanks to the internet, the bar to entry is very low. Attention spans – thanks again, internet! – are also very low. So the challenge is to go high, creating quality, memorable content. For the best results, using the optimal amount of time, here's a summary of what individuals and small businesses should do:

- **Be realistic.** The chances of going viral are incredibly slim. As seen in the Stanford University study, only 1 percent of posts have a chance at going viral.

- **Pick your spots.** It's difficult to compete with American Express, Target, John Deere, or Michelin. They will crush you. They have more resources. More name recognition. More writers. Better distribution. Pick a niche where you can be #1.

- **Be smart.** Don't post everywhere and every day. Find a time and place to post in regular intervals. Slowly build your audience and keep them with quality content. Keep your email lists for newsletters and regularly ask your viewers and readers for feedback.

- **Be original.** Everyone creates three ideas on how to sell skateboard T-shirt art online! David Spark offered this idea for tech companies producing YouTube videos. "Get a six-year-old to interview tech executives to see if they can clearly explain their product to a six-year-old."

- **Write well.** Speak directly to your audience. Add photos and video when they're well produced. Don't be afraid to be funny or original.

The Dark Side: Fake News

The biggest challenge facing publicists, the media, the public, and businesses today and in the future is the explosion of *fake news*. This is the dark side of content marketing. Fake news providers willfully produce inaccurate stories designed to promote a particular issue or candidate and/or demonize and disparage the competitor or opponent.

Americans disagree on fundamental facts, not whether Bigfoot and Elvis are meeting at the Waffle House. Of course, everyone knows they meet at Shakey's Pizza, but that's another story.

This trend had been building for years. The presidential election of 2016 demonstrated that America is divided along partisan lines, tribal lines, economic lines, geographic lines, racial lines, gender lines, and now, factual lines. Partisanship is so strong that groups can no longer agree on basic concepts of science, math, economics, and other issues. It used to be that everyone was entitled to their own opinions, but not their own facts.

This is significant. It means the end of mass persuasion. Because of the self-segregation by groups, each with its own beliefs and facts, we've entered a new era. Today we are in the age of Micro-Persuasion or Tribal Persuasion.

The news website *Gizmodo* noted in November 2016 that Facebook was the main culprit in propagating fake news. "It's hard to visit Facebook without seeing phony headlines like 'FBI Agent Suspected in Hillary Email Leaks Found Dead in Apparent Murder-Suicide' or 'Pope Francis Shocks World, Endorses Donald Trump for President, Releases

Statement' promoted by no-name news sites like the *Denver Guardian* and *Ending the Fed*."

In 2018, it was revealed that data firm Cambridge Analytica promoted fake news to promote Donald Trump during the 2016 election and harm Hillary Clinton by harvesting data from unwilling Facebook users.

According to the *New York Times*, "employees of Cambridge Analytica, eager to sell psychological profiles of American voters to political campaigns, acquired the private Facebook data of tens of millions of users – the largest known leak in Facebook history. . . . The *[London] Times* reported that people at Cambridge Analytica and its British affiliate, the SCL Group, were in contact with executives from Lukoil, the Kremlin-linked oil giant, as Cambridge built its Facebook-derived profiles. Lukoil was interested in the ways data was used to target American voters, according to two former company insiders."

CNET further explained the scandal: "Consultants working for Donald Trump's presidential campaign exploited the personal Facebook data of millions. Last month, the *New York Times* and the UK's *Guardian* and *Observer* newspapers broke news that the social networking giant was duped by researchers, who reportedly gained access to the data of millions of Facebook users and then may have misused it for political ads during the 2016 U.S. presidential election."

One reason why fake news finds a home is that trust in the media is extremely low. This opens the door for alternative news outlets. The Poynter Institute noted, "In Gallup's annual poll in 2016 measuring Americans' trust in mass media, just 32 percent of those surveyed said they had 'a great deal' or 'a fair amount' of trust in the media, down eight percentage points from 2015. Fourteen percent of Republicans surveyed expressed trust, down from 32 percent in 2016. Trust in mass media was at its highest, 72 percent, in 1976, two years after Richard Nixon resigned in the wake of the Watergate disclosures. It has fallen steadily since the early 2000s and dipped below a majority level after 2007."

Gallup concluded: "With the explosion of the mass media in recent years, especially the prevalence of blogs, vlogs, and social media, perhaps Americans decry lower standards for journalism. When opinion-driven writing becomes something like the norm, Americans may be wary of placing trust on the work of media institutions that have less rigorous reporting criteria than in the past. On the other hand, as blogs and social media 'mature,' they may improve in the American public's eyes. This could, in turn, elevate Americans' trust and confidence in the mass media as a whole."

As evidenced by the explosion of fake news on Facebook and Google, along with stories sent by email and posted on Twitter, many Americans gave the same weight to the *Denver Guardian* as they did to the *New York Times* or *Wall Street Journal*. If this doesn't depress many people, it should.

A simple internet search can show "facts" or links to "both sides" of almost any issue, any product review, service, or story, such as proof that 911 was an inside job, one product or service is significantly better than another, or Kobe Bryant is better than Michael Jordan and Lebron James combined. (Note: Kobe Bryant is the most overrated player in history. NBA analyst and former All-Star Reggie

Miller notes that Bryant is probably the 15th best player of all time.)

Traditional news outlets, like the *BBC News*, are concerned with these trends. "While the internet has enabled the sharing of knowledge in ways that previous generations could only have dreamed of, it has also provided ample proof of the line, often attributed to Winston Churchill, that 'A lie gets halfway around the world before the truth has a chance to get its pants on.'"

As the world saw during the election, with its explosion of fake stories, the truth, as the song says, is looking like a fool with its pants on the ground. In a world with different sets of beliefs and facts for different audiences, micro-targeting means different messaging for almost everything, ranging from products to services to policies to any sort of campaign from elections to referendums to what can be taught in local classrooms.

The rise of social media, with the ability to find links and stories to support any position, has intensified the problem. Michael P. Lynch, the author of "The Internet of Us: Knowing More and Understanding Less in the Age of Big Data," told the *New Yorker* magazine: "The Internet didn't create this problem, but it is exaggerating it, and it's an important and understated point. Blaming the Internet is shooting fish in a barrel – a barrel that is floating in the sea of history. It's not that you don't hit a fish; it's that the issue is the ocean. No matter the bigness of the data, the vastness of the Web, the freeness of speech, nothing could be less well settled in the twenty-first century than whether people know what they know from faith or from facts, or whether anything, in the end, can really be said to be fully proved."

In this less than brave new world, here's some advice for honest, well-meaning entrepreneurs and PR professionals:

- Don't post fake news to fake sites. Eventually (if there truly is karma) this will catch up to people and firms who do it.

- If you're the victim of a fake news story, make sure your friends, clients, and important constituents know the source of the story and that the information is bogus.

- Keep contacting legitimate news sources. There are plenty on the right, the left, the middle, and areas between the margins that care about accuracy and honesty.

- Avoid social media trolls and 24/7 commenters, most of them full of anger with plenty of time on their hands. Blocking and ignoring work best.

- Don't expect that everyone will agree with you. At best, you might reach half of an audience, and even that possibility isn't likely.

Expect that much of your information, especially if it's slightly controversial, will no longer pass the filters for the media, many groups, and the general population. Entrepreneurs, publicists, and communicators may need to create several different messages for several different groups, for every issue or product, for a very long time. Welcome to the future of content marketing.

CHAPTER 4

Measurement

*It is impossible to escape the impression
that people commonly use false standards of
measurement – that they seek power, success
and wealth for themselves
and admire them in others, and that they
underestimate what is of true value in life.*
— Sigmund Freud

*All the statistics in the world can't measure the
warmth of a smile.*
— Chris Hart

CLINT LONGLEY REPRESENTS THE TRIUMPH OF THE UN-CLUTTERED MIND.

The unknown backup quarterback for the Dallas Cowboys was glued to the bench, huddled against the cool winter chill, during the third quarter of a blowout game on November 28, 1974. The Cowboys' annual Thanksgiving contest had turned into a feast for the Washington Redskins and a turkey for the hometown crowd. Down 16–3, the Dallas fans lost all hope when All-Pro quarterback Roger Staubach was injured.

Coach Tom Landry turned away from the field and directed his steely gaze to the rookie from tiny Abilene Christian and waved him into the game. Then a funny thing happened. The longest of longshots turned from Peter Parker into Spider-Man, tossing two touchdowns while leading the Cowboys to an improbable 24–23 victory. With 28 seconds left, Longley threw a 50-yard bomb into the hands of wide receiver Drew Pearson, stealing the game. Dallas stayed alive for the playoffs, and Longley briefly passed his way into history.

Trying to explain the unlikely heroics of the backup who engineered the comeback, Cowboys guard Blaine Nye recalled, "It was the triumph of the uncluttered mind."

Measuring the Value of PR

Public relations isn't math. It's not chemistry. It's not physics. You can't measure influence or reputation like calculating the size of a neutron or the speed of an electron – there are no simple equations or measurements.

The challenge for the public relations industry is the cluttered mind. There are too many theories, too many estimates, too many experts, and too many methods. There are almost as many ways to measure the value of public relations as there are asteroids flying through our solar system.

Despite the efforts of trade groups, companies, and individuals, there's no industry standard. Businesses looking to calculate the value of their media exposure, and agencies determined to promote their worth, are locked into a cluttered marketplace of tools, tips, and transactions.

One reason for the clutter concerns the industry itself, which is marked by infighting. Hard to believe, but the PR industry doesn't always do a good job of PR. The players in measurement include:

- **Academics.** Most faculty and part-time instructors are followers. They usually accept the latest consensus platform.

- **Trade groups.** Measuring agencies such as the International Association for the Measurement and Evaluation of Communications (AMEC), the Public Relations Society of America (PRSA), and others have their own takes on measurement.

- **Private firms.** Cision, Meltwater, Carma, mediaQuant, and other companies offer services ranging from media databases and social media advice to PR measurement. Each firm presents its own proprietary software solution.

- **Sole experts.** These individuals make money from their unique platforms.

Essentially, there are two ways to measure PR: Goals and Metrics. This is extremely simplified, but true. Goals are whatever the client or organization defines. For example, if you are a college conducting a PR campaign, you might want to measure the effects of the campaign on applications, enrollments, rankings (*U.S. News & World Report*, *BusinessWeek*, etc.), or donations. A small business or corporation might want to count new business leads, sales, website traffic, etc.

But it's difficult to assign sales or donations solely to PR. Every day organizations advertise, have employees speak or attend trade shows, engage in social media marketing, and other activities. Nothing happens in a vacuum. Which leads us to metrics.

What to Measure

There are several quantitative metrics to use in measuring the impact of PR, and just as many (or more) qualitative analytics to consider. Mihaela Lica-Buter presents the basics of measuring PR in her article on Ragan.com, "10 Ways to Measure PR Results." The first class of metrics she discusses is *PR mentions*, or earned media:

- **Count media placements.** The main role of public relations is to reach out to the media to communicate a company's message. Counting media placements is one way to measure the ROI, and that can be quite significant if you get massive coverage in an array of publications. Consider how many of these mentions are mainstream or first-tier outlets (such as *TechCrunch*, *BusinessWeek*, etc.), and how many are less popular, yet highly influential. Everything that comes after these counts as a media mention, but it weighs less in terms of ROI.

- **Assess quality.** After counting, you should consider the quality of these placements: Will they influence behavioral changes in those who read them? Will these changes have a positive impact on their attitude toward your business? Are they credible? Do they feature your company exclusively? Is the tone positive? Do they convey your message accurately?

- **Measure viral impact.** Online media coverage extends to social media networks, with readers sharing news updates and reacting to them. There are several ways to measure these reactions beyond number of mentions. You should consider the number of influencers mentioning your brand, their tone of voice, and the sentiment of the message.

This is a good start. Even today, many large corporations only use the first method. One business school that I work with that's consistently ranked in the Top 25 pays two PR firms, one in the United States and one in Europe, to count media mentions. Full stories in the *Wall Street Journal, Le Monde,* or on BBC media are counted the same as one quote in the local blog. The mentions are tallied each year and compared to the number of mentions in previous years and to the competition. Before you call this method simplistic, know that many large firms do the exact same thing.

The next class of metrics that Lica-Buter discusses is *PR outcomes,* which sounds great in theory. For example, because of a series of stories placed in the media, sales jumped X percent, admissions doubled, customer retention went from negative to positive, or some similar benefit. This is the ultimate unicorn. Advertisers, marketers, business owners, academics, and entrepreneurs have been trying to link specific promotions, stories, banner ads, and other efforts to results for decades.

No matter which system is used, the results are all estimates.

Some are definitely better than others. Some include more factors, both quantitative and qualitative. Just as it's impossible to exactly define leadership, influence, humor, or why Luke Bryan and "Country Bros" are so popular, the advantages of one super-model or brand of sports car over another, PR measurement is an inexact science. Noting this in advance, here are the most common measurement systems, along with their advantages and characteristics.

Barcelona Principles Explained

The Barcelona Principles is the industry-wide solution offered by many trade groups. Here's a good explanation of the guidelines from the *PR News* website.

> The Barcelona Principles is a set of seven principles that provide the first overarching framework for effective public relations (PR) and communication measurement. The principles were originally adopted by about 200 delegates from over 30 countries at the 2nd Annual European Summit on Measurement in Barcelona, Spain, in 2010, convened by the International Association for Measurement and Evaluation of Communication (AMEC). The principles were developed with, and supported by, AMEC, the Global Alliance, the Institute for Public Relations, the International Communications Consultancy Organization, the Public Relations Consultants Association, and the Public Relations Society of America.

Several official groups with important-sounding names were involved. *PR News* continues:

> The Barcelona Principles outline the basic principles of PR and communication measurement and represent an industry-wide consensus on this topic. They are intended to not only demonstrate proof of performance, but how to foster continuous improvement. The Principles serve as a guide for practitioners to incorporate the ever-expanding media landscape into a transparent, reliable, and consistent framework. They are considered foundational in that specific measurement programs with clearly stated goals can be developed from them.

There's an implied declaration that this is the optimum solution. The experts all met and agreed, and here's the solution they produced for you. In other words, "You're welcome!"

So here are the principles along with their updates, from the official AMEC website.

Changes from the Original Barcelona Principles 2010 to the Barcelona Principles 2015

Principle 1:

- *From:* Importance of Goal Setting and Measurement
- *To:* Goal Setting and Measurement are Fundamental to Communication and Public Relations

Principle 2:

- *From:* Measuring the Effect on Outcomes is Preferred to Measuring Outputs
- *To:* Measuring Communication Outcomes is Recommended Versus Only Measuring Outputs

Principle 3:

- *From:* The Effect on Business Results Can and Should Be Measured Where Possible
- *To:* The Effect on Organizational Performance Can and Should Be Measured Where Possible

Principle 4:

- *From:* Media Measurement Requires Quantity and Quality
- *To:* Measurement and Evaluation Require Both Qualitative and Quantitative Methods

Principle 5:

- *From:* AVEs are not the Value of Public Relations
- *To:* AVEs are not the Value of Communications

Principle 6:

- *From:* Social Media Can and Should be Measured
- *To:* Social Media Can and Should be Measured Consistently with Other Media Channels

Principle 7:

- *From:* Transparency and Replicability are Paramount to Sound Measurement
- *To:* Measurement and Evaluation Should be Transparent, Consistent, and Valid

Because the seven bullet points seem a little vague, I asked for more clarification from David Rockland, the main author. Rockland proved to be a good sport about the process and seems to genuinely care about the elevation of the PR industry. He's a former Ketchum Partner and Immediate Past Chairman of the International Association for Measurement and Evaluation of Communication, and now head of Rockland Dutton Research & Consulting. Here are some excerpts from an interview conducted with Rockland from my column in Forbes in February 2016.

Can you measure PR?

Yes. You measure PR by answering one or more of the following questions: Outputs – Did you reach or engage your target audience with the messages or content you intended? Outcomes – As a result of reaching or engaging that audience, did they change in the sense of their awareness, comprehension, attitude, behavior, and/or advocacy? Organizational Results – What were the effects on the organization as a result of the changes in the audience, often measured in sales, market share, employee engagement, advocacy, donations, etc.?

If so, how can you measure PR using the Barcelona Principles?

The Barcelona Principles provide the framework for communications measurement and are not specific tools or formulas. However, by applying them, you wind up with a solid measurement program for communications. Within each Principle, there are pretty specific directions in terms of how to write measureable goals and then the techniques you apply for each type of measurement, including what are the best ways to apply those techniques. The Principles reflect the fact that communications take many different forms, and the Principles guide you in terms of how to measure each form. However, I know many companies and other types of organizations, from Southwest Airlines to Cleveland Clinic to the U.K. government, who use the Principles as the basis for their communications measurement.

One key point from the interview is this statement: "[They] are not specific tools or formulas." This is somewhat consistent with the AMEC press release, which announced: "The new AMEC framework has been deliberately developed as an interactive tool to deliver a step-by-step user process with tool tips for information and follow-on resources for the user."

The motivations for this framework were probably well-intentioned – to recognize the contributions PR makes to the reputations and bottom lines of corporations, governments, and small businesses everywhere. If the principles do nothing but elevate the value of PR and serve as a rallying cry for the industry, then they are certainly valuable. It's reasonable to assume that they consist of detailed guidelines but don't provide actual metrics.

Barcelona Principles Analyzed

Paul Senatori, Chief Analytics Officer of mediaQuant, a statistics-based media measurement company based in Portland, Oregon, deals with major corporations and small businesses. He's not a fan of the Barcelona Principles.

> They're bureaucratic, which may be appropriate when building dams or bridges or coordinating intergalactic travel, but we're talking about small organizations with limited resources and relatively low management visibility. Right out of the blocks there's nothing practical in the "principles." They're overly vague, with no concrete, analytic, or well-supported methodology.
>
> The notes and dialog from Barcelona talk extensively about linking PR to outcomes, i.e.: "You have to tie your PR projects to actual business outcomes." This reads like a 1980s *Harvard Business Review* case study. Noble and academic, but entirely impractical and self-serving, and it ignores many of the co-influences on the same outcomes.

mediaQuant earned worldwide publicity in early 2016 from a major *New York Times* article by estimating that Donald Trump received $2 billion of free publicity or airtime by appearing on live TV, print, and online news programs. They demonstrated that this earned media was more powerful than all the paid advertising of his Republican challengers. We'll discuss more on the value of advertising value equivalency (AVE) later.

Jim Sweeney, a respected PR and marketing veteran, noted in his blog that "for whatever reason, the BP [Barcelona Principles] starts with the principle of *setting goals*, which is admittedly critical, but also blatantly obvious (seriously, it's like reminding your kids to take off their clothes before they get into the bathtub). Yet the BP does not address the need for research to understand the lay of the land; to get a clear grasp of the situation, internally and externally, *before* setting goals. No primary research, no secondary research, no informal audits . . . nothing."

Ian Hood of Babel Communications in England echoed Sweeney's comments about the obvious nature of some of the principles in his blog: "The Barcelona Principles don't really take us any further forward. It's all obvious stuff that anyone with more than two active neurons ought to know already. Measuring a return from most campaigns is hard, requires a bespoke approach for the campaign in question, and, until machines understand the nuances of human communication better than humans do, is not an exact science. Agencies need to understand that and so do clients."

To better understand the metrics from a perspective outside the PR industry, I asked Loren McKechnie, Senior Manager of Online Marketing/Web Strategy & SEO for Symantec, to analyze the Barcelona Principles.

"The question that persists for me is how are third parties able to gain access to many of these metrics, as most of the important ones are not public," McKechnie says. "So benchmarking against competitors would be very difficult if not impossible with many of the web/digital advertising elements."

McKechnie was also concerned by the lack of specifics:

> I have worked for companies that spend hundreds of thousands of dollars to have "measurement" studies undertaken and delivered in fancy internal presentations. While these "fuzzy" measurement reports may justify marketing activities internally, I offer the suggestion to spend this measurement investment on understanding your buying cycle and the testing of various approaches.
>
> There are other substantial issues with external measurement. There is a market for everything. You want 10M likes on a social media website, you can get them for $.05 each. Yes there are fraud-catching algorithms touted, but the underground market is always one step ahead. As it exists in all sponsorship activities, the answers come from following the money. . . . If a relationship is symbiotic from a revenue perspective it will persist, or the vendor will start offering these metrics for sale themselves.

Advertising Value Equivalency Analyzed

One of the concerns of the Barcelona Principles involves its view on advertising value equivalency. Admittedly, AVE is just a rough estimate.

AVE has been around for many years, and there continues to be hot debate about its value. As the *New York Times* noted in a major story in 2016:

Of all the ways Donald Trump has shocked the political system, one of the most significant is how he wins primary after primary with one of the smallest campaign budgets. He still doesn't have a super PAC. He skimped on ground organization and field offices. Most important, he spent less on television advertising – typically the single biggest expenditure for a campaign – than any other major candidate, according to an analysis by SMG Delta, a firm that tracks television advertising.

The big difference between Mr. Trump and other candidates is that he is far better than any other candidate – maybe than any candidate ever – at earning media.

Over the course of the campaign, he has earned close to $2 billion worth of media attention, about twice the all-in price of the most expensive presidential campaigns in history. It is also twice the estimated $746 million that Hillary Clinton, the next best at earning media, took in. Senator Bernie Sanders has earned more media than any of the Republicans except Mr. Trump.

The mediaQuant model collects positive, neutral, and negative media mentions alike. Mr. Senatori said negative media mentions are given somewhat less weight. The best way to think of the numbers, he said, is as a gauge of which candidates are "trending" in the earned media market at any given time.

The *New York Times* story created major waves for several reasons, most of them having to do with common sense. Among the conclusions:

- Public relations is more valuable than advertising
- AVE is used by the media
- AVE is used by most people

And this doesn't even factor in the multiplier.

The Multiplier

For the uninitiated, the multiplier is a factor of how many times more valuable earned media is in terms of its impact on the viewer or reader compared to an equivalent size of advertisement or timed commercial (for example, a TV appearance lasting one minute vs. a one-minute commercial).

In an e-book written by me and published by Meltwater in 2015, I concluded, on the low side, a multiplier of five. It's an average based on academic and media studies. According to a research study by Tom Watson, "Advertising Value Equivalence – PR's Orphan Metric" (*Public Relations Review*, Volume 39, 2013):

> Although the academic approach to measurement and evaluation has mostly favored social science methodologies, there has been persistent and widespread use of advertising value equivalence (AVE) by practitioners to express the financial value

of public relations activity. The value is often boosted by multipliers which can range from 2.5 to 8.0. . . . The utility of AVE is that it is simple to calculate and suits the reporting demands of financially-driven managers and clients. Morris and Goldsworthy (2012) explain the benefits: The advantages of AVE are that it is relatively easy to calculate. . . . Indeed it represents the only cheap, quick, and easy way of putting a concrete monetary value on PR work.

Michael Levine, a well-known publicist in Los Angeles, frequent public speaker, and author of the book *Guerilla P.R.*, says, "The idea is the believability of an article versus an advertisement. Depending on how you measure and monitor an article, it is between 10 times and 100 times more valuable than an advertisement."

Here's another analogy: With advertising, you tell people how great you are; with publicity, others sing your praises. There's an old saying: Advertising is what you pay for, publicity is what you pray for. More comparisons are listed below:

- Advertising is paid, PR is earned.

- Advertising builds exposure, PR builds trust.

- Advertising creates skepticism, PR creates validation.

- Advertising is very expensive, PR is priced more moderately.

Why AVE Use Persists

Here are three reasons why AVE continues to be one of the metrics used to measure the value of public relations:

- **User experience.** You cannot divorce ads in magazines and newspapers, online, and on TV from the editorial content. Magazines, newspapers, TV, etc. try to make ads look like editorial because we've been conditioned to ignore and dismiss them. So it's logical to compare them to one another, while assuming that true editorial content is more valuable than ads.

- **Buying experience.** Every day companies, big and small, make decisions on how to transmit their messages. Do we spend our marketing budget on ads, PR, direct mail, events . . . ? We're used to comparing these options based on their perceived value and our budgets. To pretend otherwise is simply wishful thinking.

- **Apples to apples.** The market says ads are worth X for Y space in Z publication. The market has already set the price and the commodity to be compared to.

For example, in 2015 our PR firm placed a major, two-minute, sole-source feature story on CNBC for our client, Empire International Tailors of Hong Kong. For CNBC, ads cost about $10,000 per minute when the market is open. The story ran for two minutes, so the AVE was worth $20,000 × 5 = $100,000 (cost of the ad times the multiplier). The cost didn't include rebroadcasts or placement on the CNBC website.

Here's another example. For our client, Menlo College, we placed a half-page story on the front section of the *San Francisco Chronicle*. A half-page ad costs about $20,000. The PR value equaled at least $100,000, not including placement on the website.

What makes AVE more difficult to use, and PR in general harder to quantify, is content marketing. Native advertising or content that looks like earned media blurs the line between advertising and public relations and journalism. Many readers looking at stories written by journalists and articles written by the advertising department don't know the difference.

Paul Senatori offers a new phrase that offers more specificity and inserts native advertising into the equation: "A better term to assess the value of qualified earned media is media value. Media value is simply the monetized value you put on that earned media mention."

In 2016, Cision presented some insight into measurement analysis with its e-book, *Proving ROI Through Multi-Touch Attribution*, including being careful about falling in love with any one system. Cision starts with cautionary advice:

> **Understand Measurement Limitations and Complexities** – Conversions come through multiple touchpoints, they may take time, and there is not always a direct correlation. That said, determine and invest in reliable and consistent processes that measure not only traditional PR efforts, but also provide insight into current customer and market trends.

Set Yourself Up for Success – Measurement know-how is no good if there's nothing to measure. Set up tracking for all data points from your PR and marketing efforts in one place – everything from marketing campaign content and channels, to trackable PR efforts like a press release and share of voice, all the way to sales results.

mediaQuant Analysis

The blockbuster story in the *New York Times* in 2016 on measuring the media value of Donald Trump by using very simple AVE figures vaulted mediaQuant into the national spotlight. Although their analysis used but a fraction of the metrics they use for paying clients, the Trump story illustrated the value and power of public relations vs. advertising in changing perceptions and promoting issues. mediaQuant's Paul Senatori discusses the advanced metrics needed for accurate PR analysis:

> Simply knowing that you received 248 mentions in the media, or some tally of media impressions, does not tell you the relative size or magnitude of that single number. You need some analytic context. What were the minimums, maximums, and spreads within your peer group? Your interpretation of 248 mentions is very different if the peer maximum is 250 versus 2,500.
>
> PR measurement ultimately needs to move closer to the paid media measurement

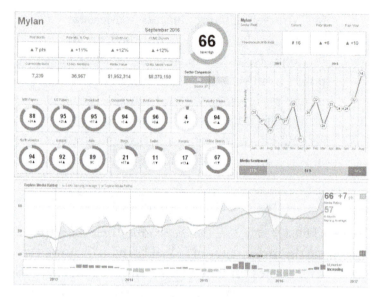

Figure 4.1. This mediaQuant dashboard illustrates the scores for Mylan Labs for September 2016. Image courtesy of mediaQuant.

model where people are the focus. It's not there yet, but the pieces are beginning to come together where there will be a fusion of earned and paid media metrics using the same underlying math. At the end of the day, all business results need to be translated into something your organization's management or funding entity understands and cares about. More often than not, that yardstick is some form of monetary currency.

The PR world can be very insular, so it's important to listen to the outside world and see what most businesses care about. Senatori notes that the challenge was turning

Pharmaceutical Brands

2 Click an Entity to see details

	Media Rating	Month Change	Mentions	Media Value	Current Rating
Johnson and Johnson	88	-2 ▼	32,254,522	$267,299,028	
Pfizer	87	+5 ▲	209,927	$3,325,690	
Valeant	76	+5 ▲	75,927	$653,440	
AstraZeneca	75	+1 ▲	47,525	$827,827	
Novartis	75	-2 ▼	68,131	$1,145,660	
Allergan	74	+4 ▲	35,662	$1,028,043	
Sanofi	73	NC	41,841	$780,531	
Teva	73	-1 ▼	35,668	$1,365,729	
Bayer HealthCare	71	+1 ▲	60,125	$834,916	
GlaxoSmithKline	71	-3 ▼	26,374	$829,536	
Roche	70	-1 ▼	24,755	$821,407	
Amgen	69	-6 ▼	27,796	$541,033	
Biogen Idec	69	+4 ▲	28,589	$542,891	
Bristol-Myers Squibb	68	+2 ▲	32,988	$185,830	
Eli Lilly	68	-2 ▼	32,599	$331,857	
Mylan	66	+7 ▲	7,239	$1,952,314	
Baxter International	64	-4 ▼	50,562	$374,538	
Janssen Pharmaceuticals	64	+1 ▲	61,613	$214,145	
Novo Nordisk	64	+9 ▲	44,060	$353,320	
Gilead Sciences	62	-7 ▼	26,747	$152,836	
Abbott	61	-3 ▼	32,870	$770,395	
Merck & Co.	61	+2 ▲	2,594	$930,110	
Celgene	60	-8 ▼	17,903	$276,633	
Takeda	59	+5 ▲	13,816	$286,404	
Actavis	58	-3 ▼	8,359	$342,497	
Shire	58	-1 ▼	6,918	$183,469	
Merck KGaA	56	+2 ▲	16,175	$72,516	
Boehringer Ingelheim	55	-2 ▼	19,221	$93,070	
Hospira	55	+5 ▲	7,667	$179,142	
Astellas	54	+1 ▲	8,219	$125,073	
Forest Laboratories	54	+3 ▲	63,080	$33,948	
Endo	53	+2 ▲	11,233	$54,389	
Regeneron Pharmaceuticals	53	+5 ▲	11,338	$60,504	
Genentech	50	-4 ▼	10,716	$150,386	

Figure 4.2. This mediaQuant dashboard compares media ratings and media value for Mylan Labs versus other brands. Image courtesy of mediaQuant.

incomprehensible data into a format or score that could be easily comprehended by clients and PR professionals alike.

Using a very simple statistic (percentile rank) we could translate all those mentions and impressions into a weighted score between 0 and 100 by media sector and segment. This resulted in a number that made sense to PR and media professionals, but had little relevance to management or others outside of the PR industry.

As an experiment, we simultaneously produced a media value or AVE metric using a combination of mentions, impressions, rating scores, sentiment values, and advertising rate tables, all at the individual mention and media segment level.

The solution, according to mediaQuant, owes as much to a diplomatic rephrasing of a term as to the power of statistics and common sense. Senatori decided to call the measurement media value.

"Today we report all metrics – mentions, impressions, ratings, and media values," says Senatori. "They all tell part of the overall media visibility story. But it's media value that tends to carry the day when communicating with a broader internal and external audience. Ask any reporter, editor, CEO, or brand or category manager to choose one of these metrics and they choose media value."

Canadian Media Ratings Points System

Media Ratings Points (MRP)

It sounds like something you heard about on The Voice involving elections segmented by demographics. But it's actually something good from Canada that people really enjoy, like Drake, Wayne Gretzky, Celine Dion, Justin Trudeau, Selena Gomez, and Tim Horton's coffee.

The updated MRP system represents a step beyond AVE and has more specificity than the Barcelona Principles. The metrics offer a combination of standardized scores (1–100) with some self-reporting. For instance, the PR professional starts by defining which criteria matter to them before they enter their media placements and mentions into the algorithm.

Here's the official explanation from the Canadian Public Relations Society (CPRS), which developed the platform.

> Media Rating Points (MRP) provides communications professionals with a widely accepted, standardized reporting platform for measuring the effectiveness of media relations campaigns. The management-by-objective system can be applied to any type of media coverage and can also be used to measure planned media campaigns, crisis communications, or unplanned, after the fact, media attention. This system can be easily customized by company or by project and provides clear metrics to evaluate media coverage and to track both total reach and cost per contact.

The measure includes:

- Editorial outlet
- Reach
- 14 standard criteria
- 10 customized criteria
- Total rating score out of 100 percent
- Cost per contact
- Audited audience reach

Users don't have to be members of CPRS. They pay an annual fee for the service: $1,700 for one user, $2,200 for two users, $3,000 for three users, and so on. The MRP creates a score for each media placement. CPRS describes its system as content analysis, since the PR professional sets the table with the criteria that are important to them, and then uses the MRP to create the scores.

Here's an example of a score of 90 from a wine maker:

Media Outlet: Tidings

Publish Date: September 30, 2012

City: National, CDN

Reach: 160,000

Brand: Stag's Leap Cabernet Sauvignon Reserve Barrel

Notes: Score 90

Tone: Positive
- ☐ Bonus / Demerit Point
- ☒ Company / Brand Mention
- ☒ Photo / Image / Logo
- ☒ Tier 1 Media Outlets
- ☒ Favorable Review/Score

The system is easy to understand, easy to explain, and somewhat easy to calculate. The downside is that it involves self-reporting, which some agencies could use to inflate the actual value of their placements. But the process is transparent.

One of the key contributions to the scholarship is the introduction of CPC, or cost per contact value. The CPC divides the total program budget or cost by the total reach.

The MRP offers this example:

Program Cost: $25,000

Total Reach: 750,000

CPC: 25,000/750,000 = $0.03

And now, the envelope please . . . Here's how CPRS calculates value:

The MRP quality score is based on the number of criteria selected (indicators) that appeared in the coverage – all selected criteria are currently weighted equally, but can be adjusted to meet campaign requirements. The ability to weight criteria based on importance to communications objectives and goals will help to provide more valid evaluation of efforts. Traditional quality indicators such as brand mention, key messaging, etc., plus custom indicators (that may be qualitative or quantitative) such as tier of media, hashtag, reporter, influence, views, engagement, etc., can be added and weighted to reflect what is of most importance to your communication objectives and outputs. *The score is out of 100 percent to easily determine how well your campaign did. It is widely considered that anything 75 percent or higher is considered a good score, and it is strongly recommended that tone is a weighted criterion in the evaluation of earned coverage.* [emphasis mine]

The Importance of Tone in Earned Communications

Tone is the explicit or strongly implicit characterization of an article's or segment's subject in earned media. Tone is one of the most critical variables in media coverage, and it can overshadow positive results on other variables.

For example, an article or segment isn't necessarily positive only because of the presence of the following variables:

- Brand
- Key message
- Spokesperson
- Call to action
- Third-party endorsement

Now here's where the MRP can be subject to interpretation – the introduction of self-reporting and qualitative measures. The MRP can still be accurate and comprehensive, but if Company X and Firm Z measure tone and the key messaging points differently, the scores for fairly similar articles will be different.

- **Ability to assign bonus points.** The system allows users to assign bonus points for exceptional impacts and outcomes. We recommend only using bonus points to increase quality score when something remarkable happens that positively impacts the results of your efforts – i.e., positive front-page coverage or lead story in top-tier media. We recommend defining criteria and number of bonus points prior to campaign launch so that it is agreed upon with stakeholders.

- **Metrics not included in quality score in MRP.** There are some standardized quantitative measures in MRP such as reach/potential audience and cost per contact – if budget is provided.

- **Unique terminology of reach in MRP.** MRP earned media reach is based on the potential audience that could be achieved in a campaign.

Besides the cost per contact or CPC, the MRP makes another unique contribution to the industry – consideration of paid media and/or content marketing. The Content Marketing Institute and social media evangelists should be very pleased. The system allows users to classify their media as paid, earned, shared, and owned.

The Canadian MRP appears to be very valuable, comprehensive, and somewhat easy to calculate. It seems to be a step or two above the Barcelona Principles. One flaw that prevents the MRP from being the MVP, at least today, concerns the many self-reporting and bonus areas that can lead to subjective results.

Measuring Social Media

Social media has provided more illusory headlines and broken dreams than the film career of Madonna, the presidential campaign of Marco Rubio, and the Hall of Fame pro football career of Johnny Manziel combined.

Earlier in this book I separated social media hype from hope, fact from fiction. While social media isn't the magical unicorn bypassing the media and leading directly to the most prized audience members promised by the management of Facebook, Twitter, Instagram, LinkedIn, and others, there's no debate about its omnipresence.

Everybody's using it. It's a valuable tool. Not a solution by itself, but very worthwhile if it's used properly.

As we discussed in a previous chapter, social media works well for crisis PR, research on products, finding reporters, creating groups, and directly responding to customers and critics. It's also a great place to watch videos of cats and to post photos of your meal or your kids on vacation, but that's another story.

Most PR professionals agree that the general method to measure social media ROI is a combination of:

- Audience reach

- Engagement

- Sentiment

Meltwater has a more specific approach, detailed in its white paper, "Social Media to Social Marketing ROI." The Meltwater formula:

1. Make sure that the social marketing effort is servicing a larger business goal.

2. Use an action-based engagement metric for the first round of tracking.

3. Follow those clicks.

4. Prompt leads to the next step of engagement.

5. Follow these leads through the funnel.

6. Report in a format that helps the boss understand success.

Basic Social Media Metrics

Vanity Metrics	Actionable Metrics
Facebook fans/reach	Likes, shares, overall engagement, fan growth rate
Traditional social media Impressions	Message amplification, social shares, mentions, syndication, additional coverage, inbound inquiries
Site traffic	Time on page, time on site, exit rate, bounce rate
Twitter followers	RT, @mention, overall engagement, follower growth rates
Number of journalists or publications in a rolodex	Press placement

Figure 4.3. Vanity metrics reflect opportunity – they measure community size. Actionable metrics reflect achievement – they measure social engagement and are therefore more valuable. Courtesy of Meltwater.

None of the software solutions from Meltwater or other sources, free or paid, are one-click, one-minute solutions. They're complex solutions that are designed to provide deep analysis on many platforms. But you need to start somewhere, so Figure 4.3 shows the basic social media metrics that matter.

Social media can also serve as an outstanding accelerator for traditional media placements. By accelerator, I mean expanding your reach beyond the original audience of the viewers or readers of the original article or story. For example, post an opinion on Twitter or Facebook. Now post a link to an article from the *Wall Street Journal* or the *Los Angeles Times* or a *CNN* video where you or your client has been interviewed. Wild guess which one will establish you or your client as an influencer. Of course, if your influence has already been established on your social media channel(s), your opinion could carry as much weight as an article that's validated by traditional media. Media intelligence tools such as Meltwater can help you track and understand the reach of your traditional media on social media as well as your growing influence.

There are two other good guidelines for PR professionals to consider when trying to measure the value of their social media efforts. The first comes from HubSpot, a company that develops and markets a product for inbound marketing along with tools for social media marketing and web analytics. According to HubSpot, you can understand the value that social media has for you by measuring the following:

- **Reach.** The number of Twitter followers, Facebook fans, LinkedIn group members, etc. that you have is directly related to your social media success. Also known as "reach," the more of it you have, the more people will see your content, spread your messages, and therefore increase your ROI. Track how your reach is increasing over time. If you're not attracting new followers as time goes on, focus more of your social media efforts on generating new fans and followers and building your reach to increase the value you get from social media marketing.

- **Traffic.** In social media marketing, one major goal you should have is to generate traffic from social media to your website and/or blog. Look at your website/blog's referral sources to determine how many visitors came from social media sites. Monitor this number over time. Are you noticing an increase in social media traffic as your reach improves?

- **Leads.** This is arguably the most important metric to use when measuring social media marketing ROI. Take another look at the traffic you're generating from social media sites. Of that traffic, how many of those website and blog visitors are converting into leads?

- **Customers.** Now take that leads data one step further. Are your social media leads actually turning into customers? And just how many of them are? Being able to attribute actual customers can be a powerful indicator that the time you're spending on social media marketing is actually worth it.

- **Conversion rate.** What's the visit-to-lead conversion rate of your social media traffic? In other words, of the social media traffic you're generating, what percentage of those visitors become leads? While this may seem like a useless metric in itself, conversion rate can be very useful when comparing one channel with another. For example, you can compare your social media conversion rate to your blogging conversion rate to analyze the ROI of those channels relative to each other.

Ragan's PR Newsletter, an outstanding source for PR news and insight, offers its own take on two ways to measure social media impact. These are:

- **Engagement vs. coverage.** It's generally agreed that the most important aspect of social media is the quality of the conversation, not the "coverage." In other words, when you measure the public relations ROI on social media, you should focus on community and conversation, rather than on number of mentions. Are people really talking about your brand, and are there influencers who carry the conversation? Is the conversation affecting your brand's social media presence?

- **Community growth.** As an effect of social conversations related to a specific PR campaign, your brand should see some growth in its own social media presence: more Twitter followers, more Facebook "likes," etc. Because "likes" and followers can be bought, though, to quantify community you must assess whether the people following or "liking" something are truly interested in your brand. Are they active users, conversing about issues related to your business? After they follow, do they participate in conversations on your social media channels?

However you decide to measure the value of your social media efforts, if you plan to benchmark your results against the results of others, remember:

- Social media can be manipulated.
- Clicks can be generated.

- Twitter followers can be purchased.
- Page views can be faked.

Starting in May 2018, Twitter suspended more than 70 million accounts, and the purge of false followers continued in June and July. The Chicago Tribune reported that "Twitter's growing campaign against bots and trolls – coming despite the risk to the company's user growth – is part of the ongoing fallout from Russia's disinformation offensive during the 2016 presidential campaign, when a St. Petersburg-based troll factory was able to use some of America's most prominent technology platforms to deceive voters on a mass scale to exacerbate social and political tensions."

Conclusions

As noted in the introduction, public relations is a social science. And public relations measurement is open to interpretation. PR measurement isn't math, chemistry, or astronomy, because so many qualitative factors need to be considered in measuring the value of PR. But we can draw some conclusions:

- Media mentions alone offer an incomplete picture.
- The Barcelona Principles are well-meaning guidelines, but not the ultimate solution.
- AVE allows for comparisons commonly used in business.
- Media value is a term worthy of further consideration.

Larger companies and organizations may have the resources to purchase systems like Carma, Cision, and

Meltwater, but the platforms can be pricey. One Fortune 100 client who attended my MED-PR media networking conference in 2018 told me her firm pays about $250,000 just to monitor the stories, mentions, tone, reach, sentiment, and other factors.

Smaller firms and individuals conducting PR campaigns may want to start with clearly defined goals, target media, use preferred messaging, and benchmark against their competitors and their previous media outreach on their own.

Although some measurement systems are better than others, they all still only provide estimates. For example, everyone can agree that media mentions is an easy-to-use metric, but it doesn't give us much information. Considering other variables, such as tone or the number of adjectives used, makes the data more accurately reflect how human beings actually respond to stimuli, although there are variations within groups and between individuals. But as the metrics require more specificity, the more open they are to interpretation.

The major story our firm placed on behalf of Menlo College, "Tiny Menlo College is Like Home for Saudi Elite," was sent to the folks at mediaQuant. It was a front-page article in the *San Francisco Chronicle*. With photos. And even more photos on the website. It was overwhelmingly positive. Based on the adjectives, mediaQuant rated it neutral (receiving neither particularly positive nor negative media mentions). I respect the mediaQuant model very much, but on this one story, we disagreed. When the client loves the story, the reporter admits it was very complimentary, and your peers in PR at Stanford University and UC-Berkeley

The Evolution of PR Measurement Complexity

LEAST COMPLEX

Counting Mentions

Counting Quotes and Full Stories

Counting Quotes and Full Sories: Comparing them to previous years and the competition

Advertising Value Equivalency (AVE)

Advertising Value Equivalency (AVE) × Multiplier

Barcelona Principles: Seven guidelines but no specific metrics

Canadian MRP: Uses AVE plus tone, reach, and other metrics (1–100 score)

mediaQuant: Uses AVE plus tone, reach, adjectives, and other metrics (1–100 score plus positive, negative, neutral)

MOST COMPLEX

Figure 4.5. PR metrics have evolved over the years, from the simple, yet useful, counting of media mentions to the most sophisticated and accurate metrics used in the Canadian MRP and mediaQuant systems.

call you in admiration to ask, "How the hell did you get such a great story?" you can probably guess it was better than neutral.

Which reminds me of work I did many years ago at USC's business school. We placed a comprehensive story in the *Wall Street Journal* about changing the name of the school from the School of Business Administration to the

Four Simple Steps to Measure Public Relations

(Conventional wisdom from Carma, Cision, Meltwater, and others.)

Set Goals and Objectives

- Create strong messaging – what do you want to say about your cause, your firm, yourself, current events, or other issues.
- Find your target audience – stockholders, voters, employees, new clients, etc.
- Agree on a desired outcome – winning an election, doubling applications, entering new markets, or another goal.

Target Your Media

- Find outlets that directly reach your audience – mainstream media, trade publications, broadcasters, newsletters, and more. An impactful story in a small publication reaching the right crowd is more powerful than a large media placement in the wrong magazine or TV show.
- Use a variety of methods to reach the media and your audience – press releases, pitches, speaking engagements, and influencer campaigns.
- Large firms may consider content marketing in major publications if they cannot create positive earned media. Small firms can create their own content in text or video.

Measure Results

- Meltwater lists Key Performance Indicators (KPIs) such as active coverage, potential reach, share of voice, social engagement, sentiment, media outreach, quality of coverage, key message penetration, earned traffic, and others.
- Carma suggests using Unique Visitors per Day (UVD) rather than Unique Visitors per Month (UVM) because it's a better metric for audience reach.
- Cision notes that it's best to measure how much coverage is being generated, the type of coverage (sentiment and messaging), and whether the campaign is reaching the right audience.

Analyze Your Competitors

- Benchmark results against yourself from last month, last year, or a similar time frame.
- Benchmark results against competitors.

Marshall School of Business, involving our new marketing plan. In typical WSJ fashion, it was about 80 to 90 percent positive, with some notes about the school's recent fall in the rankings (totally true). The story also noted some of the great programs, with some quotes about the dean, and it led readers to believe that the Marshall School was on the way up.

Almost everyone was thrilled. All except one associate dean, who focused on the negative 10 to 20 percent. Like most complainers, this dean was very loud and forwarded his complaints via email to many people. In a panic, I called a journalism professor and relayed the situation.

He replied, "Tell him he's in the *Wall Street Journal* and they spelled his name right. Be happy."

Common sense. Maybe that's the missing ingredient.

CHAPTER 5

The Top Five PR Campaigns

Publicity gets more than a little tiring. You want it, you need it, you crave it, and you're scared as hell when it stops.

— Joseph Barbera

SOMETIMES, PUBLIC RELATIONS IS THE ART OF THE IM-POSSIBLE.

Changing opinions. Promoting new products. Changing old habits. Electing the unsavory. From taste buds to popular taste, public relations can change the world. So here are five of the best, world-changing PR campaigns of all time. *PR campaigns* refers to well-coordinated, mostly well-financed, but always brilliant operations that utilized free or earned media to influence the masses to move in a certain direction – to move toward war and away from peace, to sympathize with the less fortunate, to demonize others, to visit a new location, or to accept a new habit. Compared to these difficult tasks, moving mountains isn't so difficult.

Here are my Top Five PR Campaigns of all time (in no order).

Australia Tourism
"Best Job in the World" – 2009

A help-wanted ad for a caretaker for the lonely Hamilton Island, near Queensland in Australia, turned into a massive publicity stunt. Touted as the "best job in the world," the job required no formal qualifications, just a desire to snorkel, swim, dive, and sail. For 12 hours of "work" per week, the six-month job would pay $150,000 and the employee would get to live rent-free in a villa with a pool. The campaign resulted in more than 34,000 applications and north of $200 million in free or earned media for Tourism Queensland, which sponsored the campaign. *BBC Magazine* asked, "Is This the Greatest PR Stunt Ever?" The applicants were whittled down to 12 finalists who were interviewed in Australia to determine the winner. *BBC Magazine* noted: "Tourism Queensland ticked all the boxes, creating an ongoing narrative that would work globally and gather acres of free publicity. Boasting a series of 'hooks' that began in January, from the job-application process through to the X-Factor-style whittling-down of the candidates, the campaign harnessed social media to effectively create a worldwide reality TV competition that tapped into young people's wanderlust and cleverly disguised a competition prize as a 'job.'"

Denial of Global Warming
Multiple Entities – Ongoing

Are there two sides to every issue? A coalition of energy companies and conservative groups that promote doubts about human-caused climate change used the media's habit of debating every issue to sow doubt about global warming. With echoes of the industry-funded research by tobacco companies that denied links between smoking and lung cancer, the well-coordinated PR plan has delayed new regulations for coal and petroleum industries and influenced millions of Americans. Drexel University completed a study that concluded that conservative foundations and others have bankrolled their case with $558 million between 2003 and 2010. Environmental scientist Robert J. Brulle, the Drexel study's author, said: "Powerful funders are supporting the campaign to deny scientific findings about global warming and raise public doubts about the roots and remedies of this massive global threat."

Although almost 99 percent of scientists in peer-reviewed studies conclude that human-caused pollution has contributed significantly to the rise in temperatures caused by carbon dioxide and methane emissions, and these facts are agreed upon by most governments in the world, many Americans disagree. A 2016 Pew Research study noted that beliefs differ vastly along party lines: "Seven in ten liberal Democrats (70 percent) trust climate scientists a lot to give full and accurate information about the causes of climate change, compared with just 15 percent of conservative Republicans. Some 54 percent of liberal Democrats say climate scientists understand the causes of climate change very well. This compares with only 11 percent among conservative Republicans and 19 percent among moderate/liberal Republicans."

Iraq War
U.S. Government – 2001–2003

Imagine a very unpopular president. A faltering economy. A terrorist attack on U.S. soil. The economy and stock market in a nosedive. The solution? Start a war.

To recap, on September 11, 2001, the United States was attacked when planes were hijacked and crashed on U.S. soil in New York, Pennsylvania, and Washington, DC. These attacks were blamed on Iraq. Although there was no solid evidence to link Iraq with the well-coordinated carnage, stories were fabricated to build a case for the invasion, which commenced in March 2003.

The fabrications produced by the Bush administration claimed that Iraq was involved in the 9/11 attack, Iraq colluded with Al Qaeda (the real brains behind the plane crashes), Iraq was reconstituting its nuclear program, Iraq had a new program to build and distribute chemical weapons, massive weapons of mass destruction were ready to be sent all over the world, and more. Secretary of State Colin Powell appeared at the United Nations with a fake vial of anthrax to further scare the world.

Although some reporters denied most of these false claims, enough journalists were shamed into following the party line, and by acting "patriotic," opposition to the war was muted at best. In the book *The Greatest Story Ever Sold*, *New York Times* reporter Frank Rich noted the dozens of spins and lies. His book was cited in an article in *Booklist*, produced by the American Library Association:

> In recognizing terrorist threats before 9/11, the administration launched a stream of PR distractions: Bush's Top Gun appearance on a carrier with a banner announcing "Mission Accomplished," the false packaging of Private Jessica Lynch, the blustering about uncovering administration leakers when Valerie Plame was publicly revealed as an undercover agent. Rich maintains that Bush himself was

behind the leak. By the time Hurricane Katrina devastated New Orleans, the PR spin machine that had sustained the president since 9/11 was in undeniable tatters.

Ice Bucket Challenge
Amyotrophic Lateral Scleroris (ALS) Association – 2014

Dumping ice on somebody's head used to be a prank. Now, thanks to the ALS Association, no one will ever look at an ice bucket the same way again.

Celebrities such as Bill Gates, Oprah Winfrey, Lebron James, and many others took the "challenge" to dump ice water on themselves if others would donate funds to ALS. The ice baths went viral online – not just ice baths featuring celebrities but baths featuring clever youngsters, hipsters, and families who competed for the most original bathing. *Ragan's PR Daily* notes:

> Of all the viral sensations, the Ice Bucket Challenge, which urges people to challenge their friends to donate money to the ALS Association and/or dump a bucket of ice cold water on their heads, has been the most meaningful. Since July 29, more than 1.3 million new philanthropists have donated a staggering $70 million. In the same period last year, July 29 to August 24, ALSA reports that it received $2.5 million in donations. In addition to the money, it's also brought a ton of attention to an organization with a relatively low profile. Oprah, Taylor Swift, Bill Gates, and hundreds of powerful people have donated and been doused. But ALSA

is certainly not the only worthy charity out there. The ice bucket challenge has shown us that massive amounts of people will rally around a serious disease in a fun way.

More than $115 million was raised as a result of the challenge.

Lucky Strike
Edward Bernays – American Tobacco Company – 1928

Smoking used to be cool. But only for men.

That's when Edward Bernays went to work. The "Father of Public Relations" devised a brilliant strategy for opening up a new market for the American Tobacco Company, owners of Lucky Strike cigarettes.

First he commissioned a study claiming that cigarette smoking was a method to lose weight, and he shared the results with friendly journalists. Then he piggybacked on the women's rights issue. With analogies to earning the right to vote, which women won in 1920, Bernays turned smoking into a civil rights issue.

According to the Media Institute College of Media Arts in New York, Bernays arranged for a small group of elegant young women to march in the 1929 Easter Parade in New York while smoking cigarettes. Leaving nothing to chance, he also tipped off the press, which ran photographs of the event along with opinions such as those of Miss Bertha Hunt, who noted that, "I hope that we have started something and that these torches for freedom . . . will smash the discriminatory taboo on cigarettes for women and that our sex will go on breaking down all discriminations." Smoking was suddenly a way to strike a blow for women's emancipation, and even the resulting controversy was good publicity. Within a decade more than 20 percent of women smoked cigarettes, and Lucky Strike was their brand of choice.

Here are some other fantastic PR campaigns, courtesy of Cision.

TOP PR CAMPAIGNS — A HISTORY

Volume of Press Releases

3000+

1 — 3000+

1906 2011

In **1906**, Ivy Lee created the first official press release to help the Pennsylvania Railroad release details on an electric train wreck in New Jersey. The New York Times printed it verbatim and crisis PR was born.

In the early 1920s' Edward Bernays gave Americans bacon and eggs for breakfast. He conducted a survey of **5,000 doctors** to advocate hearty protein loaded breakfasts then used the results to persuade the public to enjoy bacon and eggs.

Eat 'yer Eggs!

U.S. Egg Production

6.5 billion

Protein

1.6 billion

1919 2011

In 1938, DeBeers Mining Company engineered a PR campaign urging the public to buy diamonds by linking diamonds with romance and courtship.

Diamond Sales Explode by 55%

1938 1941

In the late **1800s**, P.T. Barnum promoted his traveling circus by sending PR agents in advance to prime newspapers.

He also invented outdoor advertising with huge **eye-catching posters**. All this led to 1873 being the banner year for circus attendance.

Coca Cola War Consumption

5 BILLION

Number of bottles of Coca-cola consumed by US troops during WWII

Breeder's Cup Tweets to Record Attendance

96,496 114,353

2009 2010

In 2010 the promoters of the Breeders' Cup Thoroughbred World Championships needed to re-invigorate interest in horse racing. They created a Twitter handle for racehorse Zenyatta and within a month Zenyatta had 1,300 Twitter followers.

Record Sales of Trivial Pursuit

To launch the new game, Trivial Pursuit, 1,800 games were sent to consumers in 1983. The company also created free game playing events in restaurants, bars and parks. The game outsold Monopoly in 1984 and Time magazine named it the "biggest phenomenon in game history".

20 Million

0 Million

1982 1984

Following the bombing of Pearl Harbor in 1941, Coca Cola persuaded the U.S. War Department that Coke was crucial to the war effort. It was announced that 'every man in uniform gets a bottle of Coca-Cola for five cents wherever he is and whatever it costs'.

INDEX

ABOUT THE AUTHORS

 **Robert Wynne** is president of the public relations and events agency Wynne Communications. He was a *Forbes* contributor on public relations from 2009 to 2018. Wynne was formerly Director of Communications at the University of Southern California's Marshall School of Business, Director of Marketing at the major law firm Manatt, Phelps & Phillips, and a reporter for *Newsweek* and the *Los Angeles Times*. He also wrote for CBS's "Walker, Texas Ranger." He has provided public relations counsel for Cornell University SC Johnson College of Business, Johns Hopkins Carey Business School, MIT Sloan School of Management, UCLA Law School, the law firm of Stroock & Stroock & Lavan, and many others. He holds a BS in Economics from Vanderbilt University and an MA in Communications from the University of Texas at Austin.

Dave Boone is a two-time Emmy and Writers Guild of America Award-winning writer. He received his Emmys as Head Writer of the 63rd and 64th Tony Awards telecasts. He's a ten-time Emmy and ten-time WGA Award nominee. He has also written for ten Academy Awards broadcasts.